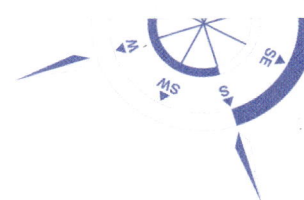

**TABLE OF CONTENTS**

## TABLE OF CONTENTS

This book is intended for use by elementary and secondary teachers, school counselors and administrators. The quotes on character, the teaching activities and bulletin board ideas are practical, applicable and easy to use or modify. Former President Theodore Roosevelt once said, "To educate a person in mind and not in morals is to educate a menace to society," while America's 16th president Abraham Lincoln wrote, "The philosophy and morals taught in the schoolhouse today will be the philosophy and morals practiced by the next generation's government." How prophetic is the wisdom of these great Americans who themselves modeled lives of virtue and noble character.

As responsible and caring educators, we are in a privileged position to help "stem the tide of moral malaise and mediocrity," for as Lincoln recognized, it is the schoolhouse where we have the opportunity and the expectation to teach virtuous principles and moral behaviors. While we are only part of the "character equation," with the home, community and businesses comprising the other essential factors, as educators we have the "power and the possibility" to help re-direct our nation's moral compass and society's well being. The future of our democracy depends on what we do or what we choose not to do with our role as character educators.

Kevin Ryan, former Director of the Center for the Advancement of Ethics at Boston University said, "Character Education is not the school's newest fad, rather it is the school's oldest mission." It provides the foundation for academic learning and moral thinking, being and doing. Character education must become a deliberate effort in our homes, schools and communities by which we come to recognize as the late Dr. Norman Vincent Peale did when he wrote, "The world is desperately in need of men and women of character who have the courage to do the right things about wrong conditions."

The quotes, activities, and ideas contained in this book can help educators deliberately plan a variety of character education activities. These activities capitalize on the daily "teachable moments" (or "character moments") we encounter as well as utilize teachers' creative resources to integrate the information into daily lessons and various classroom activities. It is hoped that principals and teachers will use the materials to help enhance the "moral ethos and climate of the school." Nationally renowned character educator and author Dr. Thomas Lickona believes that, "Character education creates the climate for learning and caring in schools."

# DEDICATION

This book is dedicated to my numerous colleagues in the Lawrence Township Schools who are "character education champions" for their students. By their words, actions and teaching, they strive to be moral examples by knowing, expecting and doing what is right and good.

It is also dedicated in loving memory of my brother, Dwight Hodgin, who was an outstanding teacher and character educator, a positive role model and inspiration for those students who were privileged to have him as their teacher. During his nearly 30-year career, he exemplified the words of one of my former colleagues who wrote, "I am a teacher, a life toucher, who affects a thousand tomorrows today (Paris Goodrum)."

*"In matters of character, example is not the main thing; it is the only thing."*
—*Albert Einstein*

**DEDICATION**

Following are some specific ideas for use of this book:

- Read or have students read the character stories, poems, inspirational readings or quotes as part of a class lesson. The stories and inspirational readings can be used for reflective writing, small group and class discussion. Use the stories and inspirational readings to have students identify the character traits or virtues within the story/reading. Have students summarize the story or reading in their own words.

  It is often a good practice, if the students are going to do reflective writing or group discussion to have copies of the story/reading for each group. Another good idea is to begin the class on Mondays and Fridays with a story or reading and take 5-10 minutes for writing or discussion. An entire class period can be used with the story/reading as well.

Using the character quotes:

- When working with younger children, paraphrase quotes so children can understand their true meaning.
- Post character quotes on the school website.
- Print character quotes in teacher and school newsletters.
- Use character quotes for student writing assignments and journals.
- Use character quotes for teacher/student discussion.
- Apply character quotes as computer screensavers.
- Encourage students to write their own character quotes, poems, bumper stickers, songs or raps.
- Decorate bulletin boards or chalkboards with character themes. Included bulletin board ideas may be enlarged and used as posters, bulletin boards, handouts or coloring sheets. The bulletin board ideas can be modified for different grade levels.
- Have students use a variety of quotes and create a character message or story.
- Have students do reports about the famous individuals who are quoted in this book and tell what dominate character traits or virtues these individuals demonstrated in their lives.
- Create a "Character Quote Collage" and ask students to bring drawings or pictures from magazines to illustrate the quotes.
- Use related character activities to help students internalize the character traits.

continued on next page

**HOW TO USE THIS BOOK**

Continued from page 5

• Encourage students to write their own or a classroom/school "character pledge" or their personal mission statement— "What I Believe."

It is my hope that you, your students and your school will benefit from the information provided and that you will recognize that effective character education is not a program nor a prescription rather it is a continuous and deliberate process and practice of expecting students to "know the good", "love the good" and have the courage to "do the right thing." May you go forth as character educators with enthusiasm and commitment and remember the importance of the words of wisdom of the writer Ralph Waldo Emerson: "People of character are the conscience of society."

**HOW TO USE THIS BOOK**

Best of Character II ★ Published by The National Center for Youth Issues ★ 1-800-477-8277 ★ www.ncyi.org

# From the Author

My second book is intended to be an extension of the original Best of Character; however, it includes a compilation of inspirational writings and poems that can be used by teachers with their students in a variety of ways. Effective character education is best done by example—adult moral modeling—and it is integrated into the curriculum and various activities of the school. It reflects the very ethos and climate of the entire school.

It is my hope that teachers will use these resources as a means to find ways to creatively and meaningfully integrate the selections and quotes into their classroom lessons through reading, reflective writing, and discussions.

*"Character education is not a program nor an event, rather it is an ongoing process of teaching by example so that students will learn to know and practice what is right and have the courage to do the right thing."*

—Duane Hodgin

**FROM THE AUTHOR**

# About the Author

**Duane E. Hodgin, Ph.D.**
Assistant Superintendent for Educational Support Services
M.S.D. of Lawrence Township

Duane Hodgin has been in public education for over 38 years serving in the Marion Community Schools, Marion, Indiana; Madison Grant High School, Fairmount, Indiana; Richmond Community Schools, Richmond, Indiana; and the M.S.D. of Lawrence Township, Indianapolis, Indiana. He has served in a variety of teaching, building level, and central office administrative positions. Three of his degrees are from Ball State University and he received his Ph. D. from Miami University in Oxford, Ohio.

In preparation for his role as a character educator, Dr. Hodgin has received special training at the Rushworth Kidder Symposium on Global Ethics, St. Louis, Missouri; the Josephson Institute of Ethics Character Counts Training, Culver City, California; the Internalizing Virtue Institute at the Center for the Advancement of Character and Ethics, Boston University, and at the Character Education Leadership Academy at the University of San Diego.

Dr. Hodgin coordinates his school district's (16,000 students) character education initiative which received the "2002 National School District of Character Award" from the Character Education Partnership in Washington, D.C. He has been a character education trainer, workshop presenter, keynote speaker, and consultant for various school districts, professional development centers, and colleges and universities in 20 states and Washington, D.C. He has done training for the Indiana Department of Education, the Indiana School Safety Specialist Academy, and the Indiana Principals Leadership Academy. Duane has also presented at local, state, regional, and national conferences on character education.

He has written various articles on character and moral education for local newspapers, professional newsletters, and the Ball State University Journal for Teaching Education. He is the co-author of a chapter in *Promising Practices in Character Education* and the author of a top selling character education resource book for teaching, *The Best of Character: Over 500 Character Quotes, Student Activities and Bulletin Board Ideas for Teachers*.

Dr. Hodgin has been the recipient of numerous educational awards and recognitions and is active in the Lawrence and Indianapolis communities. The Governor of Indiana presented him with "The Sagamore of the Wabash," the highest award that the governor can give to a citizen in Indiana.

dhodgin@msdlt.k12.in.us
(317) 423-8310/577-4021

**ABOUT THE AUTHOR**

**POEMS**

# Character

Character is who I am. It's part of me.
It's what I do and what others see.
Respect, Responsibility and genuine caring
It's serving others through helping and sharing.

Character is thinking about the things I say.
It's working with others in a cooperative way.
Honesty, Fairness, Truth and Trust
Help to bring out the good in all of us.

Character is strength and compassion, too.
It can bring out the best in me and in you.
These are universal virtues to which we can all relate.
It's a long habit continued, not dependent upon fate.

Character is encouragement, a buffer in strife.
It gives us purpose and adds meaning to life.
Character counts in all that we do.
It must matter to me and matter to you.

For, Character helps to make us whole.
It is the glue that binds our minds, spirits and souls.
Character is commitment; integrity it brings.
And it's having the courage to do the right things.

Yes, Character is part of me
It's what I do and what you see.

—Duane E. Hodgin

Best of Character II ★ Published by The National Center for Youth Issues ★ 1-800-477-8277 ★ www.ncyi.org

# The Guy in the Glass

"When you get what you want in your struggle for self
And the world makes you "King" for a day
Then go to the mirror and look at yourself
And see what that guy has to say.

For it isn't your father, or mother, or wife
Whose judgment upon you must pass
The fellow whose verdict counts most in your life
Is the guy staring back from the glass.

He's the fellow to please—never mind all the rest
For he's with you clear to the end
And you've passed your most dangerous, difficult task
If the guy in the glass is your friend.

You may be like Jack Horner and
"Chisel" a plum
And think you're a wonderful guy
But the man in the glass says you're only a bum
If you can't look him straight in the eye.

You can fool the whole world down the pathway of years
And get pats on the back as you pass,
But your final reward will be heartaches and tears
If you've cheated the guy in the glass."

—Dale Wimbrow

Citizenship

POEMS

# Don't Quit

When things go wrong, as they sometimes will,
When the road you're trudging seems all-uphill,
When the funds are low and the debts are high,
And you want to smile, but you have to sigh,
When care is pressing you down a bit—
Rest if you must, but don't quit.

Life is queer with its twists and turns,
As every one of us sometimes learns,
And many a fellow turns about
When he might have won if he had stuck it out.
Don't give up though the pace seem slow—
You may succeed with another blow.

Often the goal is nearer than
It seems to a faint and faltering man;
Often the struggler has given up
When he might have captured the victor's cup;
And he learned too late when the night came down,
How close he was to the golden crown.

Success is failure turned inside out—
The silver tint of the clouds of doubt,
And you can never tell how close you are,
It may be near when it seems afar;
So stick to the fight when you're hardest hit—
It's when things seem worse that you mustn't quit.

—Anonymous

Best of Character II ★ Published by The National Center for Youth Issues ★ 1-800-477-8277 ★ www.ncyi.org

# IF

If you can keep your head when all about you
Are losing theirs and blaming it on you,
If you can trust yourself when all men doubt you,
But make allowance for their doubting, too;
If you can wait and not be tired waiting,
Or being lied about, don't deal in lies,
Or being hated, don't give way to hating,
And yet don't look too good, nor talk too wise:

If you can dream—and not make dreams your master;
If you can think—and not make thoughts your aim,
If you can meet the Triumph and Disaster
And treat those two imposters just the same;
If you can bear to hear the truth you've spoken
Twisted by knaves to make a trap for fools,
Or watch the things you gave your life to, broken,
And stoop and build'em up with worn-out tools;

If you can make one heap of all your winnings
And risk it on one turn of pitch-and-toss,
And lose, and start again at your beginnings
And never breathe a word about your loss;
If you can force your head and nerve and sinew
To serve your turn long after they are gone,
And so hold on when there is nothing in you
Except the will, which says to them; "Hold on!"

If you can talk with crowd and keep your virtue,
Or walk with kings—nor lose the common touch,
If neither foes nor loving friends can hurt you,
If all men count with you, but none too much;
If you can fill the unforgiving minute
With sixty seconds worth of distance run,
Yours is the Earth and everything that's in it,
And—which is more—you'll be a Man, my son!

—Rudyard Kipling

**Perseverance & Determination**

**POEMS**

# IF YOU THINK . . .

If you think you are beaten, you are.
If you think you dare not, you don't.
If you'd like to win, but think you can't:
It is almost certain you won't.

If you think you'll lose, you've lost.
For out of the world we find
Success begins with a fellow's will:
It's all in the state of mind.

If you think you're outclassed, you are.
You've got to be sure of yourself before
You can ever win a prize.

Life's battles don't always go
To the stronger or faster man
But sooner or later the man who wins
Is the one who **Thinks** he can.

—Anonymous

# Lessons from an Oyster

There once was an oyster
Whose story I tell,
Who found that some sand
Had got into his shell.

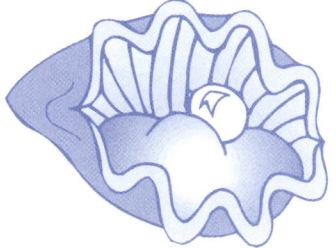
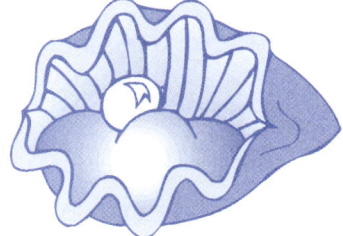

It was only a grain,
But it gave him great pain.
For oysters have feelings
Although they are so plain.

Now, did he berate
The harsh workings of fate
That had brought him
To such a deplorable state?

Did he curse at the government,
Cry for election,
And claim that the sea should
Have given him protection?

No, he said to himself,
As he lay on a shell,
Since I cannot remove it,
I shall try to improve it.

Now the years have rolled around,
As years always do,
And he came to his ultimate
Destiny do.

And the small grain of sand
That had bothered him so
Was a beautiful pearl
All richly aglow.

Now that the tale has a moral,
For isn't it grand
What an oyster can do
With a morsel of sand?

What couldn't we do
If we'd only begin
With some of the things
That get under our skin.

—Anonymous

# When Your Ego's in Bloom

Sometime when you're feeling important,
Sometime when your ego's in bloom,
Sometime when you take it for granted
You're the best qualified in the room,
Sometime when you feel that your going
Would leave an unfillable hole,
Just follow this simple instruction
And see how it humbles your soul.

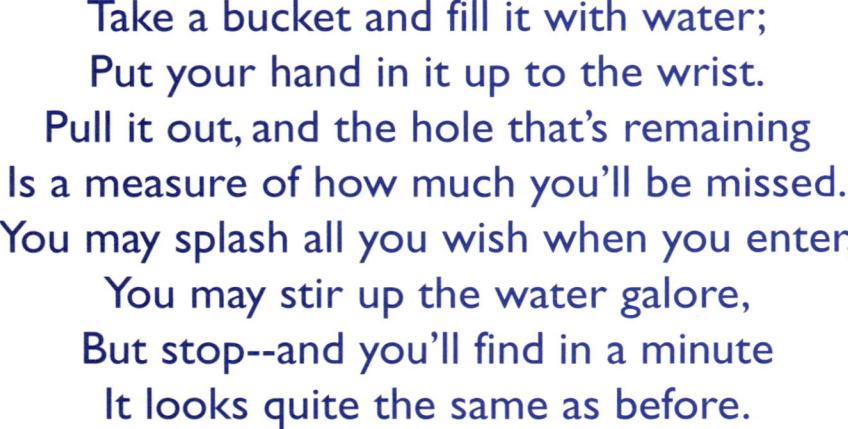

Take a bucket and fill it with water;
Put your hand in it up to the wrist.
Pull it out, and the hole that's remaining
Is a measure of how much you'll be missed.
You may splash all you wish when you enter,
You may stir up the water galore,
But stop--and you'll find in a minute
It looks quite the same as before.

The moral in the quaint example
Is just do the best you can.
Be proud of yourself, but remember,
There's no indispensable man.

—Anonymous

# Forgiveness Sets You Free
## (Edited)

From dawn till dark I carried
a big basket on my back.
Everyday I'd pick it up, like Santa and his sack.
No one asked me to transport it;
I suspect it was my pride.
Filled with righteous indignation,
the basket never left my side.

Coach is a man of poetry
who quotes from any people.
His house is almost like a church...
just without the steeple.
His advice to me was simple,
but it filled my heart with glee.
Forgiveness is the answer;
it will truly set you free.

Could it really be this easy,
just to stop and let it go?
After all the years and all the miles
could this simple trick be so?
Well, I took his words into my heart
and left my ugly sack,
Just dropped it off and walked away
and never did turn back.

The lesson's there for all who wish,
from Coach and Mother T.
Just let it go and walk away ...
forgiveness sets you free!

—Andy Hill
(Former player of Coach John Wooden, UCLA)

POEMS

# Character Poem

Respect begins with you and me.
And we must practice Responsibility.
Honesty, Fairness, Teamwork and Sharing,
That's what we mean when we talk about Caring.
Know what's right; Know what's good.
And have the Courage to do what you should.
Take Initiative in all that you do.
Make sure you can be Trusted and Persevere, too.
To have good character, I must do my part.
And I will practice the Life Skills
Using my head and my heart.

—Duane Hodgin

# Character Poem II

Character is who I am and who I choose to be.
If I'm to have good character, it's up to me.
Honesty, Respect, and Responsibility,
They help to bring out the best in you and in me.
So, where ever you go, what ever you do,
Try to make good character a part of you!

—Duane Hodgin

Best of Character II ★ Published by The National Center for Youth Issues ★ 1-800-477-8277 ★ www.ncyi.org

# THE CHAMPION

He was a young man of flesh and blood.  He wasn't made of rock.
A normal student athlete of ordinary stock.
But somehow he was different—people of character always are.
They have the courage to do what's right,
And this will take them far.

He was told to always try his best, for all efforts bring a cost.
And many times the victories came, but other times he lost.
He trained and dedicated himself; he struggled and he strained.
But he had a moral conscience that helped him make his gains.

He ran the plays repeatedly; his body became tired and sore.
Then he tells himself, "I'm not finished; I know I can do more."
And then, at last, the time had come; game time now was here.
He had to go and do his job among the boos and cheers.

And then the game was over, his body seemed to scatter.
A crowd was cheering some other, but to him it did not matter.
He turned and faced his teammates, with pride instead of shame.
He knew not that he won or lost, but that he'd played the game.

And whatever game you play, there will be struggles and strife.
But when the final score is tallied, it's how you lived your life.
It's what you do for others through respect and caring, too.
Yes, it makes a better athlete, but more importantly, a better you.

So, remember you are different.  People of character always are.
Because you have the courage to do what's right,
and this will take you far.

—Author Unknown
(Revised by Duane Hodgin)

**Courage**

**POEMS**

# Faith—Strength—Courage

The world can seem such a terrible place.
With tragedies all around.
And the prophets of doom will spread the word
Unless we take them down.
We can choose to be fearful and bitter,
And focus on all the strife.
Or, we can choose to lift up our spirits,
And take control of our life.
It is through our Faith, Strength and Courage
Which will help each of us to see;
That making any kind of difference must begin
with both you and me.
Let us think of the blessings that surround us.
Not the ones we are denied;
Think of the virtue and goodness.
And not of life's dark side.
Let us stand together for what is noble and right.
And put our differences aside,
For we are citizens of the USA
And no one can intimidate or threaten our PRIDE.
And because of our Faith—Strength—and Courage,
We will do what needs to be done.
For America is the beacon of justice and freedom,
And that makes us a nation of one.

—Duane Hodgin
(This poem was written one week after "911")

# DREAM OF FREEDOM

There's a dream in the land
With its back against the wall.
By muddled names and strange
Sometimes the dream is called.

There are those who claim
This dream for theirs alone-
A sin for which, we know,
They must atone.

Unless shared in common
Like sunlight and like air,
The dream will die for lack
Of substance anywhere.

The dream knows no frontier or tongue,
The dream no class or race.
The dream cannot be kept secure
In any one locked place.

This dream today embattled
With its back against the wall-
To save the dream for one
It must be saved for ALL.

—Langston Hughes

# God's Presence

God is present in our lives, for both you and me.
His grace and love are ever present for all of us to see.
But, if our hearts and eyes aren't open to God's loving grace,
Then we become lost and discouraged without a resting place.

God is present in our lives; however difficult things may be.
For, through His forgiveness and His healing,
He gives comfort to you and me.
If we seek and ask His help, in our times of need.
He will lift our Earthly burdens whatever they may be.

God is present in our lives. He is the candle and the light.
And His love for us can guide us through
the dark and lonely nights.
Let us see His presence
through our good times and our strife.
Knowing that He is with us every moment of our life.

—Duane E. Hodgin

Best of Character II ★ Published by The National Center for Youth Issues ★ 1-800-477-8277 ★ www.ncyi.org

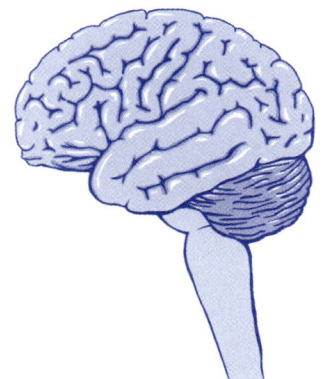

# You Choose

**Your living is determined not so much by what life brings to you as by the attitude you bring to life; not so much by what happens to you as by the way your mind looks at what happens. Circumstances and situations do color life, but you have been given the mind to choose what the color should be.**

—Anonymous

# Knowledge

Your mind is a meadow
to plant for your needs.

You are the farmer
with knowledge for seeds.

Don't leave your meadow
unplanted or bare.

Sow it with knowledge
and tend it with care.

Who'd be a know nothing
when he might grow

The seeds of knowledge
of stars and snow.

The science of numbers
the stories of time

The measure of music
the secret of rhyme

Don't be a know nothing
Plant in the spring.

And see what a harvest
The summer will bring.

—Anonymous

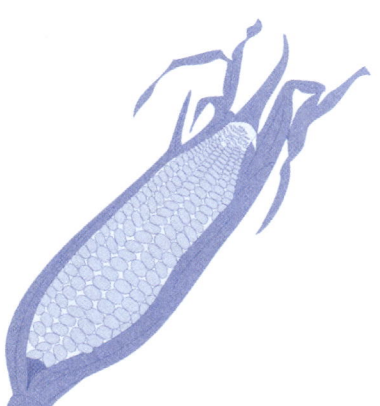

Best of Character II ★ Published by The National Center for Youth Issues ★ 1-800-477-8277 ★ www.ncyi.org

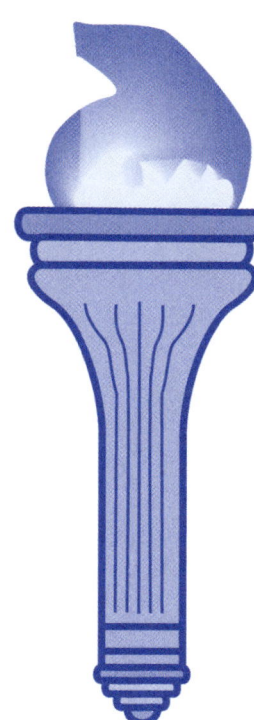

Watch your THOUGHTS:
They become WORDS

Watch your WORDS:
They become ACTIONS

Watch your ACTIONS:
They become HABITS

Watch your HABITS:
They become CHARACTER

Watch your CHARACTER:
It becomes your DESTINY

—Frank Outlaw

# Gossip

It topples companies, wrecks marriages, ruins careers, sullies reputations, Causes heartaches, nightmares, indigestion— Spawns suspicion, generates grief. Makes innocent people cry in their pillows. Even its name hisses. It's called gossip. Office gossip. Shop gossip. Party gossip. It makes headlines and headaches. Before you repeat a story, ask yourself, Is it true? Is it fair? Is it necessary? If not . . . DON'T SAY IT!

—Anonymous

# A Blueprint for Achievement

BELIEVE while others are doubting.
PLAN while others are playing.
STUDY while others are sleeping.
DECIDE while others are delaying.
PREPARE while others are daydreaming.
BEGIN while others are procrastinating.
WORK while others are wishing.
SAVE while other are wasting.
LISTEN while others are talking.
SMILE while others are pouting.
COMMEND while others are criticizing.
PERSIST while others are quitting.

—William Arthur

# You Make a Difference

Never refuse homemade brownies.
Never give anyone a fruitcake.
Remember other people's birthdays.
Sing in the shower.
Don't nap.

Don't gossip.
Don't expect money to bring you happiness.
Be forgiving of yourself and others.
Never give up on anyone miracles happen every day.
Say thanks a lot.
Say please a lot.

Take your dog to obedience school.
You'll both learn a lot.
Slow dance.
Don't rain on other people's parades.
Don't postpone joy.
Stop blaming others.
Take responsibility for every area of your life.

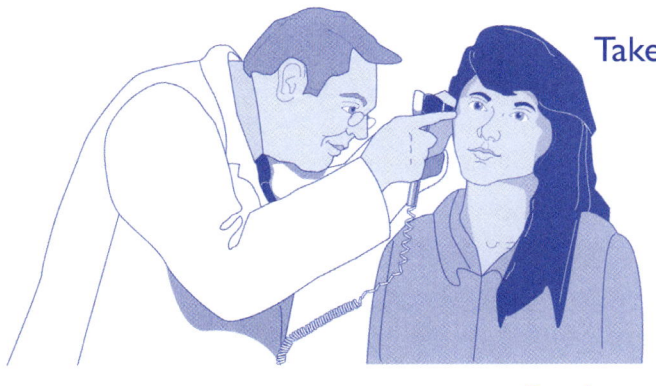

Take care of your reputation.
It's your most valuable asset.
Count your blessings.
Whistle.
Marry only for love.
Call your mother.

Do more than is expected.
Be there when people need you.
Be someone's hero.
When you care about others, when you reach out to others,
when you give of yourself to help others...

YOU MAKE A DIFFERENCE

—Anonymous

# Martin Luther King, Jr.'s Sermon

At the funeral of Martin Luther King Jr., a tape recording was played of a sermon he had once given when he talked about the kinds of things he wanted to be remembered for. Part of it went like this:

"If you get somebody to deliver the eulogy, tell them not to talk too long.

Tell them not to mention that I have a Nobel Peace Prize—it isn't important.

Tell them not to mention that I have 300-400 other awards—it's not important.

Tell them not to mention where I went to school.

I would like for somebody to mention that day that Martin Luther King, Jr. tried to give his life serving others.

I would like for somebody to say that day that Martin Luther King, Jr. tried to love somebody.

I want you to say that day that I tried to be right and to walk with them.

I want you to be able to say that day that I did try to feed the hungry.

I want you to be able to say that day that I did try in my life to clothe the naked.

I want you to say on that day that I did try in my life to visit those who were in prison.

And, I want you to say that I tried to love and serve humanity.

Yes, if you want to, say that I was a drum major. Say that I was a drum major for justice. Say that I was a drum major for peace. I was a drum major for righteousness.

And all the other shallow things will not matter ..."

Best of Character II ★ Published by The National Center for Youth Issues ★ 1-800-477-8277 ★ www.ncyi.org

# Seven Values To Live By

1. INTEGRITY
   Firm adherence to a code of moral values.

2. COURAGE
   Strength to do what is right regardless of the consequences.

3. ENTHUSIASM
   Passion for life and living.

4. HAPPINESS
   One's state of well-being, contentment and outlook on life.

5. FAITH
   Belief and trust in God

6. HOPE
   Expectations, through faith of success

7. LOVE
   Selfless concern for all others.

—Dr. Norman Vincent Peale

INSPIRATIONAL READINGS

# America, The Good Neighbor

Widespread but only partial news coverage was given recently to a remarkable editorial broadcast from Toronto by Gordon Sinclair, a Canadian television commentator. What follows is the full text of his trenchant remarks as printed in the Congressional Record:

This Canadian thinks it is time to speak up for the Americans as the most generous and possibly the least appreciated people on all the Earth. Germany, Japan and, to a lesser extent, Britain and Italy were lifted out of the debris of war by the Americans who poured in billions of dollars and forgave other billions in debts. None of these countries is today paying even the interest on its remaining debts to the United States. When France was in danger of collapsing in 1956, it was the Americans who propped it up, and their reward was to be insulted and swindled on the streets of Paris. I was there. I saw it.

When earthquakes hit distant cities, it is the United States that hurries in to help. This spring, 59 American communities were flattened by tornadoes. Nobody helped.

The Marshall Plan and the Truman Policy pumped billions of dollars into the discouraged countries. Now newspapers in those countries are writing about the decadent, warmongering Americans.

I'd like to see just one of those countries that is gloating over the erosion of the United States dollar build its own airplane. Does any other country in the world have a plane to equal the Boeing Jumbo Jet, the Lockheed Tri-Star, or the Douglas DC10? If so, why don't they fly them? Why do all the International lines except Russia fly American planes?

Why does no other land on Earth even consider putting a man or woman on the moon? You talk about Japanese technocracy, and you get

continued on next page

Continued from page 32

radios. You talk about German technocracy, and you get automobiles. You talk about American technocracy, and you find men on the moon not once, but several times—and safely home again.

You talk about scandals, and the Americans put theirs right in the store window for everybody to look at. Even their draft-dodgers are not pursued and hounded. They are here on our streets, and most of them, unless they are breaking Canadian laws, are getting American dollars from ma and pa at home to spend here.

When the railways of France, Germany, and India were breaking down through age, it was the Americans who rebuilt them. When the Pennsylvania Railroad and the New York Central went broke, nobody loaned them an old caboose. Both are still broke.

I can name you 5,000 times when the Americans raced to the help of other people in trouble. Can you name me even one time when someone else raced to the Americans in trouble? I don't think there was outside help even during the San Francisco earthquake.

Our neighbors have faced it alone, and I'm one Canadian who is tired of hearing them get kicked around. They will come out of this thing with their flag high. And when they do, they are entitled to thumb their nose at the lands that are gloating over their present troubles. I hope Canada is not one of those.

Stand proud, America!

# Life's Road Bumps

God didn't promise days without pain,
laughter without sorrow,
sun without rain,
but He did promise
strength for the day,
comfort for the tears,
and light for the way.

Disappointments are like road
bumps, they slow you down
a bit but you enjoy the
smooth road afterwards.
Don't stay on the bumps too
long. Move on!

When you feel down because you didn't
get what you want, just sit tight and be
happy, because God has thought of
something better to give you.
When something happens to you,
good or bad, consider what it means.
There's a purpose to life's events,
to teach you how to laugh more
or not to cry too hard.

—Anonymous

# Failure Is Never Final!

Failure is never final! The only time you can't afford to
fail is the very last time you try.
Failure doesn't mean I'm a failure;
it just means I haven't yet succeeded.
Failure doesn't mean I have accomplished nothing;
it just means I've learned something.
Failure doesn't mean I've been a fool;
it just means I had enough faith to experiment.
Failure doesn't mean I've been disgraced;
it just means I dared to try.
Failure doesn't mean I don't have what it takes;
it just means I must do things differently next time.
Failure doesn't mean I'm inferior;
it just means I'm not perfect.
Failure doesn't mean I've wasted my time;
it just means I have reason to start over.
Failure doesn't mean I should give up;
it just means I must try harder.
Failure doesn't mean I'll never make it;
it just means I need more patience.
Failure doesn't mean I'm wrong;
it just means I must find a better way.
Failure doesn't mean God has abandoned me;
it just means I must diligently seek His will.

—Lewis Timberlake in Timberlake Monthly

# Take Time To

### Work
it is the price of success

### Play
it is the secret of
perpetual youth

### Think
it is the source of power

### Read
it is the fountain of wisdom

### Pray
it is conversation with God

### Laugh
it is the music of the soul

### Listen
it is the pathway to
understanding

### Dream
it is hitching your wagon
to a star

### Worship
it is the highway of reverence

### Love & Be Loved
it is the gift of God

—Anonymous

# I Went to a Party, Mom

I went to a party,
and remembered what you said.
You told me not to drink, Mom
so I had a Sprite instead.

I felt proud of myself,
the way you said I would,
That I didn't drink and drive,
though some friends said I should.

I made a healthy choice,
and your advice to me was right,
the party finally ended,
and the kids drive out of sight.

I got into my car,
sure to get home in one piece,
I never knew what was coming, Mom
something I expected least.

Now I'm lying on the pavement,
And I hear the policeman say.
"The kid that caused this wreck was drunk,"
Mom, His voice seems far away.

My own blood's all around me,
as I try hard not to cry.
I can hear the paramedic say,
"This girl is going to die."

continued on next page

Continued from page 37

I'm sure the guy had no idea,
while he was flying high,
because he chose to drink and drive,
Now I would have to die.

So why do people do it, Mom
Knowing that it ruins lives?
And now the pain is cutting me,
like a hundred stabbing knives.

Tell sister not to be afraid, Mom
tell daddy to be brave,
and when I go to heaven,
put "Daddy's Girl" on my grave.

Someone should have taught him,
That it's wrong to drink and drive.
Maybe if his parents had,
I'd still be alive.

My breath is getting shorter, Mom
I'm getting really scared.
These are my final moments,
and I'm so unprepared.

I wish that you could hold me Mom,
as I lie here and die.
I wish that I could say I love you, Mom
So I love you and good-bye.

—Anonymous

Best of Character II ★ Published by The National Center for Youth Issues ★ 1-800-477-8277 ★ www.ncyi.org

# Winners Are People Like You

Winners take chances.
Like everyone else, they fear failing,
but they refuse to let fear control them.
Winners don't give up.
When life gets rough, they hang in
until the going gets better.
Winners are flexible.
They realize there is more than one way
and are willing to try others.
Winners know they are not perfect.
They respect their weaknesses
while making the most of their strengths.
Winners fall, but they don't stay down.
They stubbornly refuse to let a fall
keep them from climbing.
Winners don't blame fate for their failures
nor luck for their successes.
Winners accept responsibility for their lives.
Winners are positive thinkers who see good in all things.
From the ordinary, they make the extraordinary.
Winners believe in the path they have chosen
even when it's hard,
even when others can't see
where they are going.
Winners are patient.
They know a goal is only as worthy
as the effort that's required to achieve it.
Winners are people like you.
They make this world a better place to be.

—Nancye Sims

# The Other Guy's Opinion

Listed below are some interesting responses from students and teachers. The information was extracted from a book on motivation. The responses included are actual comments from teachers and students from "other school corporations."

However, perhaps <u>it does us all good</u> to reflect upon "the other guy's opinion" now and then.

<u>What the Students Are Saying about Their Teachers</u>

— He is really neat—he makes everything seem real.
— She really doesn't like me, so I know I'll get a lousy grade.
— He doesn't explain it so that I can understand it.
— He never has anything prepared so he just rambles on.
— I can't wait for her class. She's always teaching me things that are relevant in my life.
— Why can't they teach you something that you can use? I have taken history every year for eight years.
— Why does the coach always teach math? I understand it better than he does.
— She always plays favorites.
— He talks in a monotone; it puts me right to sleep.
— I wish he would talk less and we would do more things.
— She just gives us busy work all the time.
— There is no way I can get all that homework done. Don't they realize that I have other things to do?
— I love to go to her class. She lets you talk about things that interest you.
— He expects us to be as good an artist as he is, and we are just learning.
— He stretches a 15-minute class into two hours.
— I could read the text and take a test in one week, and learn more than I would learn a whole semester in his class.
— I swear I have taken this course three times. They just call it something different each time. That way I have to pay for it each time.
— Coaches just want to be athletes for the rest of their lives.
— He is so grouchy all the time.
— My teacher has bad breath.
— Her mind is always on something else.
— She is a piece of cake; she doesn't make you learn anything.
— He always has chalk all over his suit. I wonder if he ever gets it cleaned.
— She makes it seem so real that I feel like I'm really there.
— He gets so excited about science that I can't help but get excited too.
— He is such a push-over that all the guys are always bullying him. I don't know why he doesn't make them shape up.
— He thinks I'm so smart that I can't let him down, so I study harder than I normally would.
— He is really hard, but you sure learn a lot.
— She's never really interested in your problems.
— He always takes time to explain things so you can understand them.
— She really listens to you when you talk to her.
— If she wears that dress one more day! Can't she afford to buy anything else?

Continued from page 40

## What the Teachers Are Saying about Their Students

— Give them an inch and they take a mile.
— If you keep them busy, they won't cause you any trouble.
— I could do a good job at teaching 10 or 15 students in a class, but when it gets to be 30 or 40—forget it.
— You think nobody is listening and nobody cares and then you see a kid catch the vision and it makes it all worthwhile.
— There should be less classroom lectures and more on-the-job training.
— It's hard to get kids excited about learning any more because they are used to learning from TV and who can compete with that.
— I love to teach, but I can't do it right with so many students because I don't have time to correct all those papers and tests.
— Kids don't learn any manners at home. I spend all my time teaching things their parents should have taught them.
— All kids want to do is sit in the lunchroom with their friends and goof off.
— Some kids are so irresponsible. You depend on them to do their part and they don't.
— Kids are getting smarter each year. That means that if you don't inspire and motivate them, they can think up more mischief to get into.
— Kids have no respect for personal property.
— When kids get to college they can't spell, write, or do math. I can't understand it.
— Teaching is the most important job in the world and parents won't fight to pay teachers enough money to live on.
— Students aren't your problem—parents are.
— It seems like you spend all your time trying to motivate the underachiever and don't have time to work with the really bright kids.
— Some classes are fun and everyone learns a lot, and other classes you just can't seem to get the kids interested and excited.
— I always direct my teaching to the kids who look interested and like to participate in class.
— Kids will do anything to get your goat.
— Some days when I go to school I really fear for my life.
— We need to prepare students better for coping with today's world.
— Kids need to learn respect, courtesy, honesty, industriousness, how to get along with people, how to handle their money, how to be parents, how to buy a car, how to get a job, how to get a loan, etc.

# Greatest Love of All

I believe the children are our future.
Teach them well and let them lead the way.
Show them all the beauty they possess inside,
Give them a sense of pride to make it easier,
Let the children's laughter
Remind us how we used to be.
Everybody's searching for a hero,
People need someone to look up to
I never found anyone who fulfilled my needs,
A lonely place to be,
So I learned to depend on me.

I decided long ago
Never to walk in anyone's shadow.
If I fail, if I succeed
At least I live as I believe.
No matter what they take from me,
They <u>can't</u> take away my dignity
Because the greatest love of all
Is happening to me.
I found the greatest love of all, inside of me.

The greatest love of all is easy to achieve,
Learning to love yourself,
Is the greatest love of all.
And, if I chance that special place
That you have been dreaming of, and it
Leads you to a lonely place
Find your strength in love
Because the greatest love of all
Is happening to me
I found the greatest love of all, inside of me.

—Whitney Houston

Best of Character II ★ Published by The National Center for Youth Issues ★ 1-800-477-8277 ★ www.ncyi.org

# The Art of Friendship

The first step in the art of friendship is to be a friend, then making friends takes care of itself.

To be a friend a man should believe in the inherent goodness of other men and in their potential greatness.

To be a friend a man should strive to lift people up, not cast them down; to encourage, not discourage; to set an example that will be an inspiration to others.

To be a friend a man should practice the companionship of silence and the magic of words that his speech may build and not destroy, help and not hinder.

To be a friend a man should close his eyes to the faults of others and open them to his own.

To be a friend a man should not attempt to reform or reprimand, but should strive only to make others happy if he can.

To be a friend a man should be himself, he should be done with hypocrisy, artificiality and pretense; he should meet and mingle with people in quite simplicity and humility.

To be a friend a man should be tolerant; he should have an understanding heart and a forgiving nature, knowing that all men stumble now and then and that he who never made a mistake never accomplished anything.

To be a friend a man should go more than halfway with his fellow man; he should greet others first and not wait to be greeted; he should radiate a spirit of overflowing good will.

To be a friend a man should remember that we are human magnets; that like attracts like, and that what we give, we get.

To be a friend a man should recognize that no man knows all the answers, and that he should add each day to his knowledge of how to live the friendly way.

—Wilford A. Peterson

# The Cold Within

Six humans trapped by happenstance
In black and bitter cold
Each one possessed a stick of wood,
Or so the story's told.

Their dying fire in need of logs,
The first man held his back
For on the faces around the fire
He noticed one was black.

The next man looking cross the way
Saw one not of his church,
And couldn't bring himself to give
The fire his stick of birch.

The third one sat in tattered clothes
He gave his coat a hitch.
Why should his log be put to use
To warm the idle rich?

The rich man just sat back and thought
Of the wealth he had in store,
And how to keep what he had earned
From the lazy, shiftless poor.

The black man's face bespoke revenge
As the fire passed from his sight,
For all he saw in his stick of wood
Was a chance to spite the white.

And the last man of this forlorn group
Did not expect to gain.
Giving only to those who gave
Was how he played the game.

The logs held tight in death's still hands
Was proof of human sin.
They didn't die from the cold without,
They died from the cold within.

—Anonymous

# What Will Be Said About Your "Dash?"

I read of a man who stood to speak at the funeral of a friend. He referred to the dates on his tombstone—from the beginning to the end. He noted that first came his date of birth and spoke the following date with tears; but he said what mattered most of all was the dash between those years. (1907-1999)

For that dash represents all the time that he spent alive on Earth and now only those who loved him know what that little line is worth. For it matters not, how much we own; the cars, the house, the cash, what matters is how we live and love and how we spend our dash.

So think about this long and hard—are there things you'd like to change? For you never know how much time is left, that can still be rearranged. If we could just slow down enough to consider what's true and real, and always try to understand the way other people feel.

And be less quick to anger, and show appreciation more and love the people in our lives like we've never loved before. If we treat each other with respect, and more often with a smile, remembering that this special dash might only last a little while.

So, when your eulogy's being read with your life's actions to rehash, would you be proud of the things they say about how you spent your dash?

—Anonymous

# Children Learn What They Live

If children live with criticism,
They learn to condemn.

If children live with hostility,
They learn to fight.

If children live with ridicule,
They learn to be shy.

If children live with shame,
They learn to feel guilty.

If children live with tolerance,
They learn to be patient.

If children live with encouragement,
They learn confidence.

If children live with praise,
They learn to appreciate.

If children live with fairness,
They learn justice.

If children live with security,
They learn to have faith.

If children live with approval,
They learn to like themselves.

If children live with acceptance and friendship,
They learn to find love in the world.

—Dorothy Law Nolte

Best of Character II ★ Published by The National Center for Youth Issues ★ 1-800-477-8277 ★ www.ncyi.org

# Respect

**R**   is for respect toward others and yourself.

**E**   is for equality—everyone is equal in one way or another.

**S**   is for special because everyone is special in their own way.

**P**   is for positive because if you are positive you will earn respect.

**E**   is for excellence. If you give your best, you will become the best.

**C**   is for caring—not just for ourselves and others but for everything around us, including our Earth.

**T**   is for the togetherness that makes us one. We should have respect for the world around us and everyone.

Respect is to give your best. Not to be better than the rest. Just to know that you tried. Then you should be satisfied. It's like riding a bike. Every once in a while you fall, but that's all right as long as you give it your all. Respect is to give, not to hold to yourself. You should spread it around and share it with everyone else.

—Browney Wilkes
—From a Canadian Newspaper

# Celebrate Life!

In this special moment in Life . . .
Think freely. Practice patience.
Smile often. Savor special moments.
Live God's message. Make new friends.
Rediscover old ones. Feel deeply.
Tell those you love that you do.
Forget trouble. Forgive an enemy.
GROW. Hope. Be Crazy.
Count your blessings.
Observe miracles. Make them happen.
Discard worry. Give. Give in.
Trust enough to take.
Pick some flowers. Share them.
Keep a promise. Look for rainbows.
Gaze at stars. See beauty everywhere!
Work hard. Be wise. Try to understand.
Take time for people.
Make time for yourself.
Laugh heartily. Spread joy. Take a chance.
Reach out. Let someone in.
Try something new. Slow down.
Be soft sometimes.
BELIEVE IN YOURSELF.
Trust others. See a sunrise.
Listen to rain. Reminisce.
Cry when you need to. Trust life.
Have faith. Enjoy wonder.
Comfort a friend. Save good ideas.
Make some mistakes. Learn from them.
CELEBRATE LIFE!

—Author Unknown

# A S...hip

One day, when I was a freshman in high school, I saw a kid from my class walking home from school. His name was Kyle. It looked like he was carrying all of his books. I thought to myself, "Why would anyone bring home all his books on a Friday? He must really be a nerd."

I had quite a weekend planned (parties and a football game with my friends tomorrow afternoon), so I shrugged my shoulders and went on.

As I was walking, I saw a bunch of kids running toward him. They ran at him, knocking all his books out of his arms, and tripping him so he landed in the dirt. His glasses went flying, and I saw them land in the grass about ten feet from him. He looked up and I saw this terrible sadness in his eyes.

My heart went out to him. So, I jogged over to him and as he crawled around looking for his glasses, I saw a tear in his eye. As I handed him his glasses, I said, "Those guys are jerks. They really should get lives." He looked at me and said, "Hey, thanks!" There was a big smile on his face. It was one of those smiles that showed real gratitude.

I helped him pick up his books, and asked him where he lived. As it turned out, he lived near me, so I asked him why I had never seen him before. He said he had gone to private school before now.

I would have never hung out with a private school kid before. We talked all the way home, and I carried some of his books. He turned out to be a pretty cool kid. I asked him if he wanted to play a little football with my friends. He said, "yes." We hung out all weekend and the more I got to know Kyle, the more I liked him, and my friends thought the same of him.

continued on next page

Continued from page 49

Monday morning came, and there was Kyle with the huge stack of books again. I stopped him and said, "Boy, you are gonna really build some serious muscles with this pile of books everyday!" He just laughed and handed me half the books.

Over the next four years, Kyle and I became best friends. When we were seniors, we began to think about college. Kyle decided on Georgetown, and I was going to Duke. I knew that we would always be friends, that the miles would never be a problem. He was going to be a doctor, and I was going for business on a football scholarship.

Kyle was valedictorian of our class. I teased him all the time about being a nerd. He had to prepare a speech for graduation.

I was so glad it wasn't me having to get up there and speak. Graduation day, I saw Kyle. He looked great. He was one of those guys that really found himself during high school. He filled out and actually looked good in glasses. He had more dates than I had and all the girls loved him. Boy, sometimes I was jealous.

Today was one of those days. I could see that he was nervous about his speech. So, I smacked him on the back and said, "Hey, big guy, you'll be great!" He looked at me with one of those looks (the really grateful one) and smiled. "Thanks," he said.

As he started his speech, he cleared his throat, and began, "Graduation is a time to thank those who helped you make it through those tough years. Your parents, your teachers, your siblings, maybe a coach ... but mostly your friends. I am here to tell all of you that being a friend to someone is the best gift you can give them. I am going to tell you a story."

I just looked at my friend with disbelief as he told the story of the first day we met. He had planned to kill himself over the weekend.

Continued from page 50

He talked of how he had cleaned out his locker so his Mom wouldn't have to do it later and was carrying his stuff home. He looked hard at me and gave me a little smile.

"Thankfully, I was saved. My friend saved me from doing the unspeakable."

I heard the gasp go through the crowd as this handsome, popular boy told us all about his weakest moment. I saw his mom and dad looking at me and smiling that same grateful smile. Not until that moment did I realize its depth.

Never underestimate the power of your actions. With one small gesture, you can change a person's life. For better or for worse.

God puts us all in each other's lives to impact one another in some way. Look for God in others.

—Author Unknown

# All I Ever Really Need to Know I Learned In Kindergarten

Most of what I really need to know about how to live, what to do, and how to be, I learned in kindergarten. Wisdom was not at the top of the graduate school mountain, but there in the sandbox at nursery school.

These are the things I learned: Share everything. Play fair. Don't hit people. Put things back where you found them. Clean up your own mess. Don't take things that aren't yours. Say you're sorry when you hurt somebody. Wash your hands before you eat. Flush. Warm cookies and cold milk are good for you. Live a balanced life. Learn some and think some and draw and paint and sing and dance and play and work every day some.

Take a nap every afternoon. When you go out into the world, watch for traffic, hold hands, and stick together. Be aware of wonder. Remember the little seed in the plastic cup. The roots go down and the plant goes up and nobody really knows how or why, but we are all like that.

Goldfish and hamsters and white mice and even the little seed in the plastic cup—they all die. So do we.

And then, remember the book about Dick and Jane and the first word you learned, the biggest word of all: LOOK. Everything you need to know is in there somewhere. The Golden Rule and love and basic sanitation, ecology and politics and sane living.

Think of what a better world it would be if we all—the whole world— had cookies and milk about 3 o'clock every afternoon and then lay down with our blankets for a nap. Or if we had a basic policy in our nation and other nations to always put things back where we found them and clean up our own messes. And it is still true, no matter how old you are, when you go out into the world, it is best to hold hands and stick together.

—Robert Fulghum

Best of Character II ★ Published by The National Center for Youth Issues ★ 1-800-477-8277 ★ www.ncyi.org

# The Art of Giving

The art of giving encompasses many areas.

Emerson said it well: "Rings and jewels are not gifts, but apologies for gifts. The only true gift is a portion of thyself."

We give of ourselves when we give gifts of the heart: love, kindness, joy, understanding, sympathy, forgiveness.

We give of ourselves when we give gifts of the mind: ideas, dreams, purposes, ideals, principles, plans, inventions, projects, poetry.

We give of ourselves when we give gifts of the spirit: prayer, beauty, aspiration, faith.

We give of ourselves when we give the gift of time: patience, attention, consideration.

We give of ourselves when we give the gift of words: encouragement, inspiration, guidance.

The finest gift a man can give to his age and time is the gift of a constructive and creative life.

— Wilferd A. Peterson

# Your First Break

**Do You Remember Who Gave You Your First Break?**

Someone saw something in you once.
That's partly why you are where you are today.
It could have been a thoughtful parent, a perceptive teacher,
a demanding drill sergeant, an appreciative employer,
or just a friend who dug down in his pocket and came up
with a few bucks.
Whoever it was, had the kindness and the foresight to
bet on your future.
Those are two beautiful qualities that separate the human
being from the orangutan.
In the next 24 hours, take 10 minutes to write a grateful
note to the person who helped you.
You'll keep a wonderful friendship alive.
Matter of fact, take another 10 minutes to give somebody
else a break.
Who knows?
Someday you might get a nice letter.
It could be one of the most gratifying messages
you ever read.

—Reprint from the "Wall Street Journal"

Best of Character II ★ Published by The National Center for Youth Issues ★ 1-800-477-8277 ★ www.ncyi.org

# Ten Lessons for Living and Caring

First:  Learn to remember names. A person's name is very important to an individual. You compliment a person by remembering names.

Second:  Be a comfortable kind of individual so there is no strain in being with you.

Third:  Acquire the quality of relaxed easy-goingness so that people also feel relaxed with you.

Fourth:  Don't be egotistical. Guard against giving the impression you know it all. Be natural and genuinely humble.

Fifth:  Cultivate friendships with hopeful, positive people.

Sixth:  Eliminate the factors from your personality which tend to turn people off.

Seventh:  Heal every misunderstanding you have had or now have. Drain off your grievances and forget them.

Eighth:  Practice liking people until you learn to do so genuinely.

Ninth:  Never miss an opportunity to say a word of commendation upon anyone's achievement, or express sympathy in sorrow or disappointment.

Tenth:  Get an upbeat quality to your personality, one that gives inspiration to other people.

—Dr. Norman Vincent Peale

# Lots of Things to be Happy About

*It is the "little things" in our lives, that we often take for granted, that can bring us those special moments and simple joys.*

—Duane Hodgin

- Awakening to a "new day."
- Seeing the sun set.
- Seeing the moon rise.
- The "snuggle right in" feeling.
- Canoeing down a peaceful river on a beautiful day.
- Whitewater rafting on "any day."
- The feel of a rug under bare feet.
- Your dog that greets you when you come home.
- Your cat that "snuggles next to you when he's ready."
- Babies who never cry.
- Moderation
- An athletic contest going into "overtime or extra innings."
- A smile.
- A hug from a friend or colleague.
- A note of thanks or appreciation.
- Elvis (The legend lives!).
- Reruns of "I Love Lucy," "Andy Griffith and Barney," "The Three Stooges."
- Starting to make things happen.
- God's grace and love.
- Healing.
- A movie that makes you feel good or provokes thought.
- A smell of burning logs in a fireplace.
- The smell of burning leaves in the autumn.
- The first snowfall.
- "Talking or hanging-out" with a friend.
- Donuts (your preference, of course).
- Large biceps.
- Competence.
- The smell of homemade soup or bread.
- People, books or movies who make you laugh.
- Country music and country line dancing.

continued on next page

Continued from page 56

- Christmas morning
- "Doing something special for someone else because you want to."
- Passing notes during church (of course, kids only).
- A music box that plays, "Somewhere My Love."
- Stopping being a "perfectionist."
- Being able to "let things go."
- Feeling "an inner peace."
- Roasting hot dogs and marshmallows on a bonfire.
- Shopping
- A sunny, winter day.
- Birds singing.
- A walk in the woods.
- A loving family and supportive, caring friends and colleagues.
- A job.
- Your health.
- Your faith.
- True, lasting values
- Grandparents
- Respect
- Your favorite CD's or cassette tapes.
- "Breaking for rainbows."
- "Do not disturb" signs.
- The smell of fresh cut grass and fresh cut flowers.
- Walking over crunching leaves.
- Borders and Barnes & Noble book stores.
- Having a "roof party" for friends and neighbors.
- Your child's "good report card."
- "Not worrying" about "what might happen."
- Pizza
- A new car
- Inspirational and motivational quotes.
- Reading a good book in your favorite place.
- An act of kindness (received or extended).
- One size fits all.

—Adopted from *14,000 Things To Be Happy About* and edited by Duane Hodgin, with a few personal notes added.

# Rules for Being Human

1. You will receive a body. You may like it or hate it, but it will be yours for the entire period this time around.

2. You will learn lessons. You are enrolled in a full-time informal school called LIFE. Each day in this school, you will have the opportunity to learn lessons. You may like the lessons or think they are irrelevant and stupid.

3. There are no mistakes, only lessons. Growth is a process of trial and error; experimentation. The "failed" experiments are as much a part of the process as the experiment that ultimately "works."

4. A lesson is repeated until learned. A lesson will be presented to you in various forms until you have learned it. When you have learned it, you can then go on to the next lesson.

5. Learning lessons does not end. Every part of life contains its lesson. If you are alive, there are always lessons to be learned.

6. "There" is no better than "here." When your "there" has become a "here," you will simply obtain another "there" that will again, look better than "here."

7. Others are merely mirrors of you. You have all the tools and resources you need. What you do with them is up to you. The choice is yours.

8. What you make of your life is up to you.

9. Your answers lie inside you. The answers to LIFE'S questions lie inside you. All you need to do is look, listen, and trust.

10. You will forget all this.

11. You can remember it whenever you want.

—Anonymous

# Attitude

The longer I live, the more I realize the impact
of attitude on life.
Attitude to me, is more important than facts.
It is more important than the past,
than education,
than money,
than circumstances,
than failures,
than success,
than what other people think
or say or do.

It is more important than appearance,
giftedness or skill
It will make or break a company . . .
a church . . . a home.

The remarkable thing is we have a choice
everyday regarding the attitude we will
embrace for that day.

We cannot change our past . . .
we cannot change the fact that people will
act in a certain way.
We cannot change the inevitable.
The only thing we can do is play on the one
string we have,
and that is our attitude . . .
I am convinced that life is 10%
what happens to me
and 90% how I react to it.
And so it is with you . . .

—Charles Swindoll

**Courage**

**INSPIRATIONAL READINGS**

# Sanibel Dreams

If I Had My Life to Live Over I Would

Relax, take things less seriously
Climb more mountains
Eat more ice cream and fudge
Have fewer imaginary problems
Take care of real problems
Have great moments, instead of hopes of great years
Have success be a journey, not a goal

Walk barefoot on the beach
Love more . . . . . . . . Hate less
Do a good deed for the joy of it
Be less critical
Live to die . . . . . . . not die to live
Laugh more heartily
Admire youth, even with envy

Chance more mistakes
Ride more merry-go-rounds
Rather give, than get
Be born old . . . . . . . to get young
To know sooner, these are truths

Wish I could say I live the above,
but alas, I have human frailties

—Harold Austin

# Colin Powell's Rules

1.  It's not as bad as you think . . . it will look better in the morning.

2.  Get mad; then get over it.

3.  Avoid having your ego so close to your position that when your position falls, your ego goes with it.

4.  It can be done!

5.  Be careful what you choose—you may get it.

6.  Don't let adverse facts stand in the way of a good decision.

7.  You can't make someone else's choices. You shouldn't let someone else make yours.

8.  Check small things.

9.  Share credit.

10. Remain calm. Be kind.

11. Have a vision. Be demanding.

12. Don't take counsel of your fears or nay sayers.

13. Perpetual optimism is a force multiplier.

# Napoleon Hill's Tips for Developing Positive Attitudes

1.  Recognize that your mental attitude is the one and only thing over which you, and you alone, have complete control, and exercise the privilege of taking possession of and directing your mind with a positive mental attitude.

2.  Select the person who, in your opinion, is the finest person in all the world, past or present, and make that person your pacemaker for all your life's activities.

3.  Form the habit of saying or doing something every day which will make another person or persons feel better. You can do this by a phone call, a kind word in passing, dropping a postal card, or by doing some other kindness for another.

4.  Keep a daily diary of your good deeds in behalf of others, and never let the sun set on a single day without recording some act of human kindness.

5.  Adopt the habit of having a good laugh when you become angry or irritated.

6.  Accept all criticism as an opportunity for self-examination.

7.  Refuse to permit yourself to worry.

8.  If you're feeling sorry for yourself, find someone who is worse off than you are and help that person.

9.  If you have objectionable habits which you wish to break, show yourself who is boss by abstaining from such habits for one month.

10. Understand that one can hurt your feelings, make you angry or frighten you without your full cooperation and consent, and therefore determine to close your mind to all who endeavor to enter it for destructive purposes.

11. Learn the art of mastering your emotions by exercising them under only conditions of your own choosing.

continued on next page

Continued from page 62

12. Form the habit of tolerance. Keep an open mind on all subjects and toward people of all races and creeds. Become more patient and generous with others.

13. Make yourself understand that it isn't defeat which whips you, but your mental attitude toward it. Then train yourself to look for the seed of equivalent benefit in each defeat which may come your way.

14. Learn to close your mind to all the failures and unpleasant circumstances of the past.

15. Realize, and prove to your own satisfaction, that every adversity, failure, defeat, sorrow and unpleasant circumstance, whether of your own making or otherwise, carries with it the seed of an equivalent benefit which may be transmuted into a blessing of great proportions.

—Napoleon Hill

**Justice & Fairness**

**INSPIRATIONAL READINGS**

# To "Let Go" Takes Love

To "let go" does not mean to stop caring, it means, I can't do it for someone else.

To "let go" is not to cut myself off, it is the realization I can't control another.

To "let go" is not to enable, but to allow learning from natural consequences.

To "let go" is to admit powerlessness, which means the outcome is not in my hands.

To "let go" is not to try to change or blame another, it is to make the most of myself.

To "let go" is not to care for, but to care about.

To "let go" is not to fix, but to be supportive.

To "let go" is not to judge, but to allow another to be a human being.

To "let go" is not to be in the middle arranging all the outcomes, but to allow others to affect their own destinies.

To "let go" is not to be protective, it is to permit another to face reality.

To "let go" is not to nag, scold or argue, but instead to search out my own shortcomings and to correct them.

To "let go" is not to adjust everything to my desires, but to take each day as it comes, and cherish myself in it.

To "let go" is not to criticize and regulate anybody, but to try to become what I dream I can be.

To "let go" is not to regret the past, but to grow and to live for the future.

To "let go" is to fear less and to love more.

—Author Unknown

Best of Character II ★ Published by The National Center for Youth Issues ★ 1-800-477-8277 ★ www.ncyi.org

STORIES

# I Taught Them All
# (Reflections of a Teacher)

I have taught in high school for over 10 years!

During that time I have given assignments, among others, to a murderer, an evangelist, a pugilist, a thief, and an imbecile.

The murderer was a quiet little boy who sat on the front seat and regarded me with pale blue eyes; the evangelist, easily the most popular boy in school, had the lead in the junior play; the pugilist lounged by the window and let loose at intervals a raucous laugh that startled even the geraniums; the thief was a gay-hearted lad with a song on his lips; the imbecile was a soft eyed little animal seeking the shadows!

The murderer awaits death in the state penitentiary, the evangelist has lain a year now in the village churchyard; the pugilist lost an eye in a brawl in Hong Kong; the thief, by standing on tiptoe, can see the windows of my room from the county jail; and the once gentle-eyed little moron beats his head against a padded wall in the state mental hospital.

All of these pupils once sat in my room, sat and looked at me gravely across worn brown desks. I must have been a great help to those pupils—I taught them the rhyming scheme of the Elizabethan sonnet and how to diagram a complex sentence!

—Anonymous
The Clearing House (1937)

**Responsibility**

**STORIES**

# Our Mission

Our deepest fear is not that we are inadequate. Our deepest fear is that we are powerful beyond measure. It is our light, not our darkness, that most frightens us.

We ask ourselves, who am I to be brilliant, gorgeous, talented and fabulous? Actually, who are you not to be?
You are a child of God.
Your playing small doesn't serve the world.
There is nothing enlightened about shrinking
so that other people
won't feel insecure around you.

We are born to manifest the Glory of God that is within us.
It's not just in some of us, it's in everyone, and
as we let our own light shine, we consciously give other
people permission to do the same.
As we are liberated from our own fear, our presence
automatically liberates others.

—Nelson Mandella

# THAT BOY

Once there was a boy I always saw on my way to school. He looked about seven or eight years old. He was always on the side of the road. When I walked by him, I always said "Hi!" with a big smile on my face. Everyday that little boy would look at me grin then say "HELLO!" I never knew why that little boy was on the road in front of his house. Until, one day I asked him. He said looking down as if he was ashamed and said, "My mom is an alcoholic. When she comes home, I always get out of her way. She has hurt me before, but I know she doesn't mean it. So, I usually go outside." I looked at the boy and saw the sadness in his eyes. The boy spoke again. "Everyday when you go by and say 'Hi!' and smile, it gives me a sense of feeling in my heart. Everyday I look forward to that little thing in my life which is all I really look forward to. I would like to thank you for all those times you made me feel better." That day I learned that such little things can make a difference in someone's life.

—Ashley Cox

STORIES

# Dad's T.V.

I came home from school one day.

As usual my dad was in the living room watching T.V.

I asked him if he would help me with my homework.

He said "No." So I did my homework alone.

I asked him if he would like to play basketball.

He said "No, can't you see I am watching T.V."

So I went outside and shot hoops alone.

Then when I came inside, because it was getting dark.

I asked dad if he wanted to go out to eat.

As usual, he said, "No." So I ate a chicken sandwich all alone.

What does my dad see in those talk shows?

I have no clue, but he is stuck to the T.V. just like glue.

Then I asked if he would come and tuck me in for bed.

Guess what he said? "No." So I went to bed on my own.

When I got up the next morning, I found him already

in front of the T.V. I said good morning but I got no response.

Now I understand. It's plain to see that my dad would

rather have his T.V. than me.

—Amanda Plank, 1997

Best of Character II ★ Published by The National Center for Youth Issues ★ 1-800-477-8277 ★ www.ncyi.org

# The Starfish Story

One day walking along the shore, a teacher and a student came upon a beach littered with thousands of storm-tossed starfish, writhing and dying in the hot sun. Without a word, the teacher scooped up a starfish and gently deposited it in the waves. Overwhelmed by the sheer multitude of the suffering creatures, the student just stood and watched as the teacher picked up another starfish, and yet another, releasing them in the healing safety of the cool green water. At last, the student spoke. "Teacher, what is the use in even trying? There are too many. How can you make any difference?" The teacher lifted another starfish from the burning sand and carried it into the surf to set it free, then turned to the student. "I made a difference to that one."

—Author Unknown

# 1,000 Marbles

The older I get, the more I enjoy Saturday mornings. Perhaps it is the quiet solitude that comes with being the first to rise, or maybe it is the unbounded joy of not having to be at work. Either way, the first few hours of a Saturday morning are most enjoyable.

A few weeks ago, I was shuffling toward the kitchen with a steaming cup of coffee in one hand and the morning paper in the other. What began as a typical Saturday morning turned into one of those lessons that life seems to hand you from time to time. Let me tell you about it.

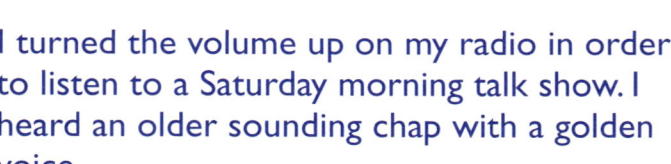

I turned the volume up on my radio in order to listen to a Saturday morning talk show. I heard an older sounding chap with a golden voice.

You know the kind, he sounded like he should be in the broadcasting business himself.

He was talking about "a thousand marbles" to someone named Tom. I was intrigued and sat down to listen to what he had to say.

"Well, Tom, it sure sounds like you're busy with your job. I'm sure they pay you well, but it is a shame you have to be away from home and your family so much. Hard to believe a young fellow should have to work sixty or seventy hours a week to make ends meet. Too bad you missed your daughter's dance recital."

He continued, "Let me tell you something, Tom, something that has helped me keep a good perspective on my own priorities."

Continued on next page

Continued from page 72

And that's when he began to explain his theory of a "thousand marbles."

"You see, I sat down one day and did a little arithmetic. The average person lives about 75 years. I know, some live more and some live less, but on average, folks live about 75 years."

"Now then, I multiplied 75 times 52 and I came up with 3,900 which is the number of Saturdays that the average person has in their entire lifetime. Now stick with me, Tom, I'm getting to the important part."

"It took me until I was 55 years old to think about all this in any detail," he went on, "and by that time I had lived through over 2,800 Saturdays. I got to thinking that if I lived to be seventy-five, I only had about a thousand of them left to enjoy."

"So I went to a toy store and bought every single marble they had. I ended up having to visit three toy stores to round up 1,000 marbles. I took them home and put them inside of a large, clear plastic container right here in my workshop next to the radio. Every Saturday since then, I have taken one marble out and thrown it away."

"I found that by watching the marbles diminish, I focused more on the really important things in life. There is nothing like watching your time here on this earth run out to help get your priorities straight."

"Now let me tell you one last thing before I sign-off with you and take my lovely wife out for breakfast. This morning, I took the very last marble out of the container. I figure if I make it until next Saturday then God has blessed me with a little extra time to be with my loved ones . . . ."

Continued on next page

Continued from page 73

"It was nice to talk to you, Tom. I hope you spend more time with your loved ones, and I hope to meet you again someday. Have a good morning!"

You could have heard a pin drop when he finished. Even the show's moderator didn't have anything to say for a few moments. I guess he gave us all a lot to think about. I had planned to do some work that morning, then go to the gym. Instead, I went upstairs and woke my wife up with a kiss. "C'mon honey, I'm taking you and the kids to breakfast."

"What brought this on?" she asked with a smile. "Oh, nothing special," I said. "It has just been a long time since we spent a Saturday together with the kids. Hey, can we stop at a toy store while we're out? I need to buy some marbles."

**HAVE A GREAT WEEKEND AND MAY ALL SATURDAYS BE SPECIAL AND MAY YOU HAVE MANY HAPPY YEARS AFTER YOU LOSE ALL YOUR MARBLES.**

—Author Unknown

# Three letters from Teddy

Teddy's letter came today, and now that I have read it, I will place it in my cedar chest with the other things that have been important to me during my life as a teacher.

The letter began . . . "Dear Miss Thompson: I wanted you to be the first to know." I smiled as I read the words that he had written and my heart swelled with the pride that I had no right to feel. Let me reminisce to 16 years ago. I have not seen Teddy Stallard since he was a student in my fifth grade class. It was early in my career and I had only been teaching a few years.

From the first day that he stepped into my classroom I disliked Teddy. Teachers, although everyone knows differently, are not supposed to have favorites in a class but most especially that are not to show dislike for any child. There wasn't a child that I particularly liked that year, but Teddy was most assuredly the one that I disliked.

He was dirty, not just occasionally, but all the time. His hair hung low over his face, and he actually had to pull it out of his eyes as he wrote his papers in class. And this was even before it was fashionable to do so. Too, he had a peculiar odor about him that I could never identify.

His physical faults were many and his intellect left a lot to be desired. By the end of the first week, I knew he was hopelessly behind the others. Not only was he behind; he was just plain slow. I began to withdraw from him immediately. In fact, I just concentrated on my best students and let the others follow along as best they could. Teddy fell into this group.

While I did not actually ridicule Teddy, my attitude was obviously quite apparent to the class, for he quickly became the "class goat," the "outcast," the "unlovable," and the "untouchable." He knew that I didn't like him, but he didn't know why. All I knew is that he was a little boy that no one cared about and I made no effort on his behalf.

As the Christmas holidays approached, I knew that Teddy would never catch up in time to be promoted to the next grade level. He would be a repeater.

Continued on next page

Continued from page 75

To justify myself, I went to his cumulative folder from time to time. He had very low grades for the first four years, but no grade failure. How he had made it I didn't know. I closed my mind to the personal remarks that I read in his folder: In the first grade the teacher had written, "Teddy shows promise by work and attitude, but he has a poor home situation." Second grade: "Teddy could do better; mother terminally ill. He receives little help at home." Third grade, the teacher wrote: "Teddy is a pleasant boy, helpful, but too serious. Slow learner. Mother passed away at the end of the year. Teddy has been affected greatly by her death." Fourth grade: "Very slow but well behaved. Seems sad most of the time. Unfortunately, father shows no interest in Teddy." Well, I said to myself, they passed him four times, but he will certainly repeat fifth grade. "Do him good," I said to myself.

It was time for our annual Christmas party. Teachers always get several gifts at Christmas but mine that year seemed bigger and more elaborate than ever. I did make sure that Teddy's gift was not the last one I picked up: In fact, it was in the middle of the pile. It's wrapping was a brown paper bag and on it he had colored Christmas trees and bells all over it. It was stuck together with masking tape.

"For Miss Thompson from Teddy," it read. The group was completely silent, and for the first time I felt conspicuous, embarrassed, because they all stood watching me unwrap the gift. As I removed the last bit of masking tape, two items fell to my desk. A gaudy rhinestone bracelet with several stones missing and a small bottle of dime store cologne, half empty. I could hear the snickers and whispers and I wasn't sure that I could look at Teddy. When my eyes did meet his, I saw the hurt in his eyes.

"Isn't this lovely," I asked, placing the bracelet on my wrist. "Teddy, would you help me fasten it." He smiled shyly as he fixed the clasp and I held up my wrist for all of them to admire. There were a few hesitant ahs, but as I dabbed the cologne behind my ears and remarked how good it smelled, all the little girls lined up for a dab behind their ears as well.

After the party the children filed out with shouts of "See you next year and Merry Christmas," but Teddy lingered at his desk. When they had all left he walked toward me, clutching his little gift and books to his chest. With his sad eyes he looked at me and said, "You smell just like mom used to smell, when she was alive." He said softly, "Her bracelet looks real pretty on you too. I'm glad you liked it." He left quickly. I locked the door, sat down at my desk and wept. Resolving to make up to Teddy what I had deliberately deprived him of—a teacher who cared.

Continued on next page

Continued from page 76

After Christmas vacation, I stayed nearly every day after school to help him. Slowly but surely he caught up with the rest of his class. Gradually there was a definite upward curve in his grades, and it was obvious that he was going to pass the fifth grade. Something I thought impossible only a few months ago.

I did not hear from Teddy until eight years later, when his first letter appeared in my mail box. Dear Miss Thompson, I just wanted you to be the first to know, I will be graduating second in my high school class next month. Very truly yours, Teddy Stallard.

I sent him a card of congratulations and a small package of a pen and pencil gift set. I wondered what he would do after graduation. Four years later Teddy's second letter came. Dear Miss Thompson: I wanted you to be the first to know, I was just informed that I will be graduating first in my class. The University has not been easy, but I did like it. Very truly yours, Teddy Stallard.

I sent him a good pair of sterling silver monogrammed cuff links and a card. I was so proud of him that I could burst. And now today, nearly 22 years after I had him in my class, Teddy's third letter arrived. Dear Miss Thompson, I wanted you to be the first to know, as of today, I am Theodore J. Stallard, M.D. How about that!!?? I am going to be married in July, the 27th to be exact. I wanted to ask if you could come and sit where mom would have sit if she were here. I'll have no family there since my dad died last year. Very truly yours, Ted Stallard, M.D.

I am not sure what kind of gift one sends to a doctor on completion of medical school and State Boards. Maybe I'll just wait and take a wedding gift. But my note can't wait. Dear Ted, Congratulations! You made it, and you did it yourself! In spite of those like me and because of us, this day has come for you. God bless you. I will be at that wedding with bells on. Sincerely, Elizabeth Thompson Ballard.

Perhaps this message says to us that as teachers "what we do and what we say each and every day or what we fail to do and what we fail to say" does, in no small way truly make a significant difference for the children whose lives we touch.

—Anonymous

# Life Is What You Make It and How You Take It

The 92-year-old, petite, well-poised and proud lady, who is fully dressed each morning by eight o'clock, with her hair fashionably coifed and makeup perfectly applied, even though she is legally blind, moved to a nursing home today. Her husband of 70 years recently passed away, making the move necessary. After many hours of waiting patiently in the lobby of the nursing home, she smiled sweetly when told her room was ready. As she maneuvered her walker to the elevator, I provided a visual description of her tiny room, including the eyelet sheets that had been hung on her window. "I love it," she stated with enthusiasm of an 8 year old having just been presented with a new puppy. "Mrs. Jones," I said, "you haven't seen the room. Just wait."

"That doesn't have anything to do with it," she replied. "Happiness is something you decide ahead of time. Whether I like my room or not doesn't depend on how the furniture is arranged . . . it's how I arrange my mind."

"I already decided to love it . . . . It's a decision I make every morning when I wake up. I have a choice; I can spend the day in bed recounting the difficulty I have with the parts of my body that no longer work, or get out of bed and be thankful for the ones that do. Each day is a gift, and as long as my eyes open I'll focus on the new day and all the happy memories I've stored away . . . just for this time is my life."

Old age is like a bank account . . . you withdraw from what you've put in. So, my advice to you would be to deposit a lot of happiness in the bank account of memories and thank you for your part in filling my Memory Bank. I am still depositing!

—Anonymous

QUOTES

"In any moment of decision, the best thing you can do is the right thing."

—Theodore Roosevelt

"Character is about internal struggles between what I ought to do and what I want to do."

—Russell Gough

"Character is knowing what is right, thinking about what is right, practicing what is right, and having the courage to do the right thing."

—Duane Hodgin

"Character is not about the left or the right, rather it is about what is right."

—Robert Chase

"Remember always that you not only have the right to be an individual, you have an obligation to be one."

—Eleanor Roosevelt

"Be more aware of your responsibilities than you rights."

—Anonymous

QUOTES

**Responsibility**

**QUOTES**

"Our life is a gift; our character is our choice"
—Duane Hodgin

"The purpose of an education is to make choices clear to people, not make the choices for people."
—Peter McWilliams

"Always put off until tomorrow what you shouldn't do at all."
—Morris Mandel

"The ultimate measure of a man is not where he stands in moments of comfort, but where he stands at times of challenge and controversy."
—Martin Luther King, Jr.

"Our character is the sum total of all our everyday choices."
—Margaret Jensin

**"What everyone else is doing is quite irrelevant when it comes to doing what is right."**

—Russell Gough

**"You are capable of becoming what you are capable of becoming if you are willing to do what you need to do."**
—Duane Hodgin

**"Character is not hereditary."**

—Thomas Jefferson

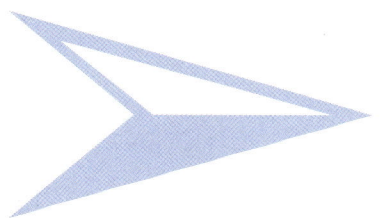

**"Life is a gift. Freedom is a responsibility."**

—Eric Schaulb

**"Hold yourself responsible for a higher standard than anyone expects of you."**

—Henry Ward Beecher

"Only you can decide how you are going to act."

—Anonymous

"Freedom does not include freedom from responsibility."

—Margaret Thatcher

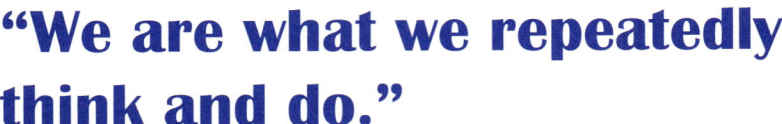

"We are what we repeatedly think and do."

—Anonymous

"Dare to do the right thing."

—Duane Hodgin

"No one is free who is not a master of himself."

—Claudius

"Keep doing what is right, and you can't do wrong."

—Anonymous

"You only live once, but if you live it right, once is enough."

—Joe E. Lewis

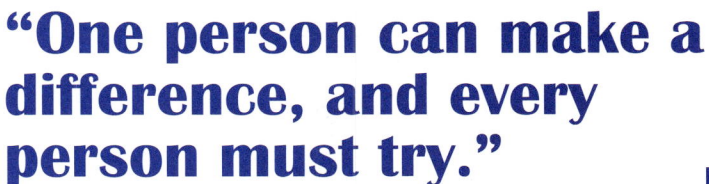

"There is so much benefit in doing the right thing in a world where there is often too many low expectations."

—Michael Josephson

"One person can make a difference, and every person must try."

—John F. Kennedy

"The only ones among you who will be really happy are those who will have sought and found how to serve."

—Albert Schweitzer

"The greatest reward is not what we receive for our labor, but what we become of it."

—John Reska

QUOTES

"The climate of the school is determined by the 'Character Connection'—what the staff and students do and say and how they do and say it."

—Duane Hodgin

"Character is more important than knowledge or ability. It is the glue that holds the fabric of an organization and a society together."

—Duane Hodgin

"The purpose of life involves caring about and service to others."

—Duane Hodgin

"People of character help to create schools of character."

—Duane Hodgin

"The end of all education should surely be service to others."

—Cesar Chavez

"There is nothing more unequal than equal treatment of unequal people in unequal situations."

—Duane Hodgin

"People of character are the conscience of society."
—Ralph Waldo Emerson

"A nation, as a society, forms a moral person, and every member of it is personally responsible for his society."

—Thomas Jefferson

"We are only angels with one wing.  We can only fly while embracing each other."
—Luciano de Crescenzo

"Life is a place of service, and in that service one has to suffer a great deal that is hard to bear, but more often to experience a great deal of joy. But that joy can be real only if people look upon their lives as a service and have a definite object in life outside themselves and their personal happiness."
—Leo Tolstoy

"Aim for service, not success. Success will follow."

—Anonymous

QUOTES

"The life of a nation is secure only while the nation is honest, truthful and just."

—Frederick Douglas

"The truest friend to the liberty of his country is he who tries to promote its virtue."

—Samuel Adams

"Citizenship consists in the service of the country."

—Jawaharlal Nehru

"Do your duty in all things. You cannot do more; you should never wish to do less."

—Robert E. Lee

"Patriotism is loyalty to friends, people, families."

—Robert Santos

"The purpose of life involves caring about and service to others."

—Duane Hodgin

Best of Character II ★ Published by The National Center for Youth Issues ★ 1-800-477-8277 ★ www.ncyi.org

"No one can predict what heights you can soar. Even you will not know until you spread your wings."

—Anonymous

"Life does not require us to be the biggest or the best. It only asks that we try."

—Anonymous

"Persevere. Sometimes we have to be on our backs before we can look up."

—Duane Hodgin

"There is no reward without effort."

—Deb Brown

"If there's no wind, row."

—Anonymous

"The only place success comes before sweat is in the dictionary."

—Anonymous

"There are two ways to get to the top of an oak tree – climb the branches or sit on an acorn and wait."

—Deb Brown

"Fall seven times. Stand up eight."

—Japanese Proverb

"Without struggle, there can be no progress."

—Frederick Douglas

"You can go a long way after you are tired."

—Deb Brown

"Ability is what you're capable of doing. Motivation determines what you do. Attitude determines how well you do it."

—Lou Holtz

Best of Character II ★ Published by The National Center for Youth Issues ★ 1-800-477-8277 ★ www.ncyi.org

"**Character and perseverance conquer all things.**"

—Duane Hodgin

"**You can do what you have to do, and sometimes you can do it even better than you think you can.**"

—Jimmy Carter

"**Perseverance and courage are two major benchmark's of one's strength of character.**"

—Duane Hodgin

"**Never give up on anyone, miracles happen everyday.**"

—H. Jackson Brown

"**The difference between ordinary and extraordinary is that little extra.**"

—Anonymous

**"One may go a long way after one is tired."**

—French Proverb

**"Difficult things take a long time, impossible things a little longer."**

—Anonymous

**"It's not that I'm so smart, it's just that I stay with problems longer."**

—Albert Einstein

**"Consider the postage stamp: its usefulness consists in the ability to stick to one thing till it gets there."**

—Josh Billings

**"The difference between perseverance and obstinacy is that one comes from a strong will, and the other from a strong won't."**

—Henry Ward Beecher

Best of Character II ★ Published by The National Center for Youth Issues ★ 1-800-477-8277 ★ www.ncyi.org

"Respect—It begins or ends with you and me."

—Duane Hodgin

"There is no respect for others without humility in one's self."

—Henri Frederic Amiel

"Respect for ourselves guides our morals; respect for others guides our manners."

—Laurence Sterne

"Probably no greater honor can come to any man than the respect of his colleagues."

—Cary Grant

QUOTES

"They cannot take away our self-respect if we do not give it to them."

—Mahatma Ghandi

"It is better to deserve honors and not have them than to have them and not deserve them."

—Mark Twain

"Our character is like a mirror which constantly reflects who you are, how you behave, what you believe, and what others believe about you."

—Duane Hodgin

"Children need role models more than critics."

—Joubert

"What is on the inside of you is more important than what is on the outside of you; nurture the good."

—Deb Brown

"The greatest reward is not what we receive for our labor, but what we become by it."
—John Ruskin

"People are like stained-glass windows. They sparkle and shine when the sun is out, but when the darkness sets in, their true beauty is revealed only if there is a light from within."

—Elizabeth Rubler Ross

"The respect others reward you is in exact proportion to the respect you reward yourself."

—Rusty Berkus

"It is true that I am only one, but I am one. The fact that I cannot do everything will not prevent me from doing what I can."

—Edward Everett Hale

"Of all the properties that belong to honorable men, not one is so highly prized as character."

—Henry Clay

"You cannot consistently perform in a manner that is inconsistent with the way you see yourself."

—Zig Ziglar

"Strive not to be a success, but rather to be of value."

—Albert Einstein

"Self-respect permeates every aspect of your life."

—Joe Clark

"We must build a new world, a far better world—one in which the eternal dignity of man is respected."

—Harry S. Truman

"Dignity does not consist in possessing honors, but in deserving them."

—Aristotle

"Respect for self and others is the foundation of all human interaction and relationships."

—Duane Hodgin

"The best place to find a helping hand is at the end of your arm."

—Swedish Proverb

"No act of kindness, no matter how small, is ever wasted."

—Aesop

"Great thoughts always come from the heart."

—Marquis de Vauvenargues

"Be nice to nerds. There is a good chance you'll end up working for one someday."

—Deb Brown

"Kindness is the chain by which society is bound together."

—Goethe

"We can do no great things—only small things with great love."

—Mother Teresa

QUOTES

"The key words in character are Care and Act."

—Duane Hodgin

"Small acts of kindness can create large feelings of joy."

—Duane Hodgin

"The philosophy of life can be summed up in two words: Be kind!"

—Anonymous

"Kind words can be short and easy to speak, but their echoes are truly endless."

—Mother Teresa

"Reach out and touch someone with a hug, a smile, a kind deed and encouraging words."

—Duane Hodgin

"It's always nice to be nice."

—Anonymous

"Caring is the wellspring of the soul."

—Duane Hodgin

"You can have your 'high-tech' and your 'hardware,' but it is better to have the soft touch that says, 'I care.'"

—Duane Hodgin

Best of Character II ★ Published by The National Center for Youth Issues ★ 1-800-477-8277 ★ www.ncyi.org

"You cannot do a kindness too soon because you never know how soon it will be too late."

—Ralph Waldo Emerson

"A really great person is the person who makes every person feel great!"

—G.K. Chesterton

"If you want others to be happy, practice compassion. If you want to be happy, practice compassion."

– Dalai Lama

"Teach this triple truth to all: A generous heart, kind speech, and a life of service and compassion are the things which renew humanity."

—Buddha

"What wisdom can you find that is greater than kindness?"

—Rousseau

"The gardens of kindness never fade."

—Greek Proverb

QUOTES

"**Character is not doing what you have a right to do, but doing what is right.**"

—John Naber

"**In our land of give and take, there are too few people willing to give what it takes.**"

—Clebe McClary

QUOTES

Life shrinks or expands in proportion to one's courage."

—Anais Nin

"**The world is desperately in need of men and women of character who have the courage to do the right things about wrong conditions.**"

—Norman Vincent Peale

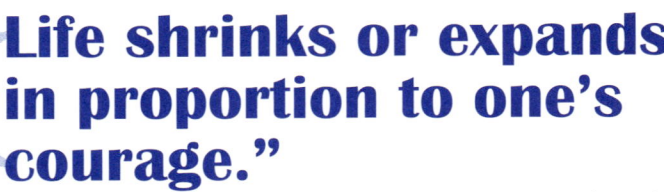

"**Success is not measured by what you get or do in life, but what you do for others.**"

—Anonymous

Best of Character II ★ Published by The National Center for Youth Issues ★ 1-800-477-8277 ★ www.ncyi.org

## "Don't do what's easy; do what's right!"

—Deb Brown

## "One's strength of character stands the test of time."

—Anonymous

## "You cannot become who you should be, if you don't do what you should do."

—Anonymous

## "Always do the right thing. This will gratify some people and amaze the rest."

—Mark Twain

## "The bravest thing you can do when you are not brave is to profess courage and act accordingly."

– Corra Harris

## "The only courage that matters is the kind that gets you from one moment to the next."

—Mignon McLaughlin

## "Courage is very important. Like a muscle, it is strengthened by use."

—Ruth Gordon

**"Courage is meeting and living each new day the best you can, whatever the circumstances."** —Duane Hodgin

**"Character is having the courage to do what you know you should do when you don't want to do it."**

—Duane Hodgin

**"To stand alone for what is right is one of life's most noble and courageous deeds."** —Duane Hodgin

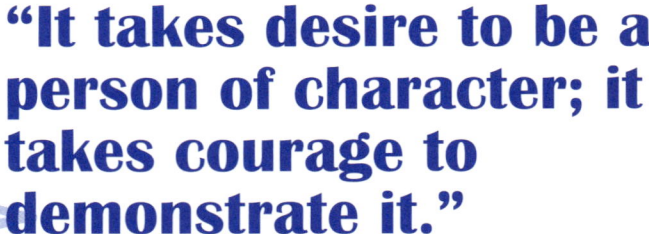

**"It takes desire to be a person of character; it takes courage to demonstrate it."** —Duane Hodgin

**"Our strength of character is in direct proportion of our willingness to demonstrate the courage to do the right thing."** —Duane Hodgin

"Most of us are proud of our freedom to say what we please. What we wish we had is the courage to say it."

—Anonymous

"Morality may consist solely in the courage of making a choice."

—Lean Blum

"Courage is a gift. Those who have it never know for sure whether they have it until the test comes."

—Carl Sandburg

"One man with courage makes a majority."

—Andrew Jackson

"The truth of the matter is we most always know the right thing to do. The hard part is doing it."

—Norman Schwarzkopf

"Few delights can equal the mere presence of one whom we trust utterly."

—George MacDonald

"As soon as you trust yourself, you will know how to live."

—Goethe

"Trust your gut instinct ... but reject your first reaction."

—Anonymous

"You may be deceived if you trust too much, but you will live in torment unless you trust enough."

—Frank Crane

"Self-trust is the first secret of success."

—Ralph Waldo Emerson

"Say what you mean and mean what you say."

—Deb Brown

"Few things help an individual more than to place responsibility upon him, and to let him know that you trust him."

—Booker T. Washington

"To be trusted is a greater compliment than to be loved."

—George MacDonald

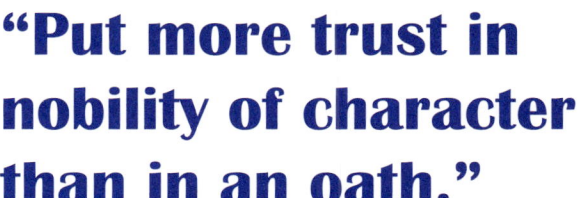

"One must be fond of people and trust them if one is not to make a mess of life."

—E.M. Forster

"Put more trust in nobility of character than in an oath."

—Solon

"If people trust and love you, you will never walk alone."

—Philippos

"What loneliness is more lonely than distrust?"

—T.S. Eliot

"It is impossible to go through life without trust: that is to be imprisoned in the worst cell of all, oneself."

—Graham Greene

"Self-trust is the essence of heroism."

—Ralph Waldo Emerson

"The best proof of love is trust."

—Dr. Joyce Brothers

"The only way to make a man trustworthy is to trust him."

—Henry L. Stimson

"A person who trusts no one can't be trusted."

—Jerome Blattner

"To be trusted is a greater compliment than to be loved."

—George MacDonald

"If you can't trust yourself, then who are you going to turn to when you need advice?"

—Chris Anderson

"Trust men and they will be true to you;

—Ralph Waldo Emerson

"Love God and trust your feelings. Be loyal to them. Don't betray them."

—Robert C. Pollock

"Every kind of peaceful cooperation among men is primarily based on mutual trust and only secondary on institutions such as courts of justice and police."

—Albert Einstein

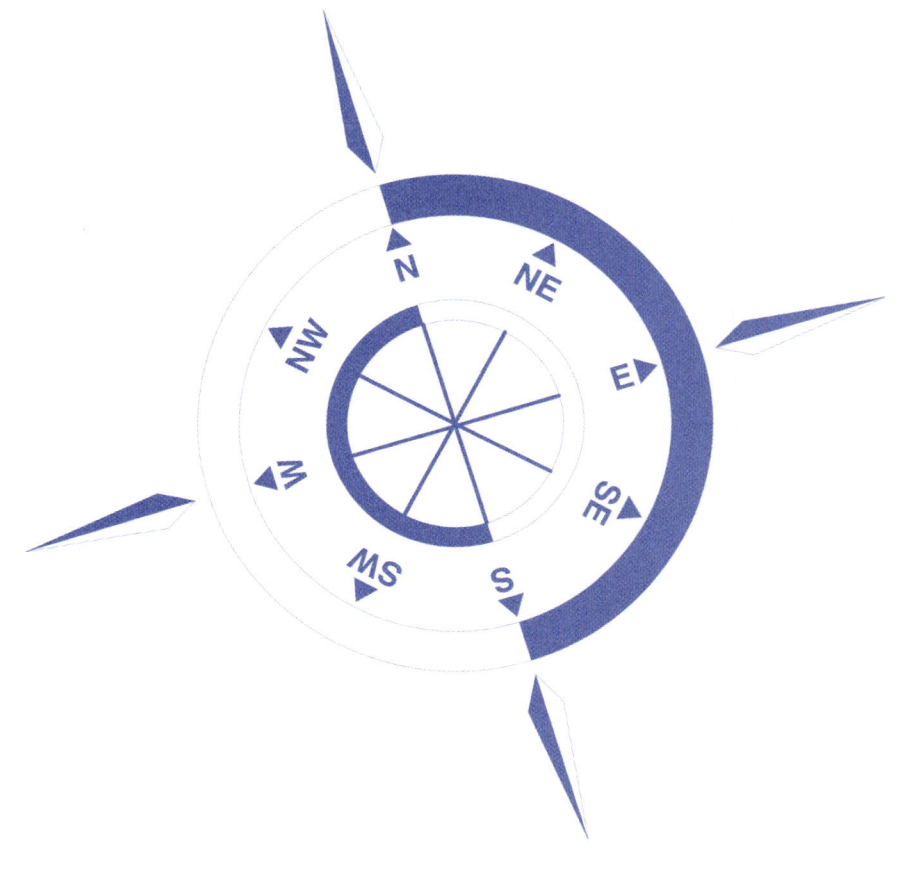

# Into The Light

Under darkness each child stands,
As if a tree does shelter them,
From the light that knowledge gives.
Each mind, a sapling,
Requires light to live.
And you, the teacher,
An Autumn's Breeze;
With each passing through the trees
More light through the branches reach.
Enlightened are all those you teach.
With a strong parental root,
Upward towards brightness,
The sapling soon will shoot.

— Leslie Stone

# We Believe

**Responsibility**

**Teachers and Teaching**

We believe this is a place
where ALL kids are first
and none are last.

We practice the mission
and preach the cause.

We protect the innocent
and promote forgiveness.

We are what we profess.

We love our children
and accept their needs.

We acknowledge their failure
and commend their success.

We celebrate their uniqueness.

We like what we do
and need each other to learn.

We share a time and a place together.

We enjoy our relationships.

We have succeeded at both achievement
and citizenship.

We believe this is a place where ALL kids are first and none
are last.

—Anonymous

Best of Character II ★ Published by The National Center for Youth Issues ★ 1-800-477-8277 ★ www.ncyi.org

# A HUNDRED YEARS FROM NOW IT WILL NOT MATTER WHAT MY BANK ACCOUNT WAS, THE SORT OF HOUSE I LIVED IN, OR THE KIND OF CAR I DROVE —BUT THE WORLD MAY BE DIFFERENT BECAUSE I WAS IMPORTANT IN THE LIFE OF A CHILD.

—Anonymous

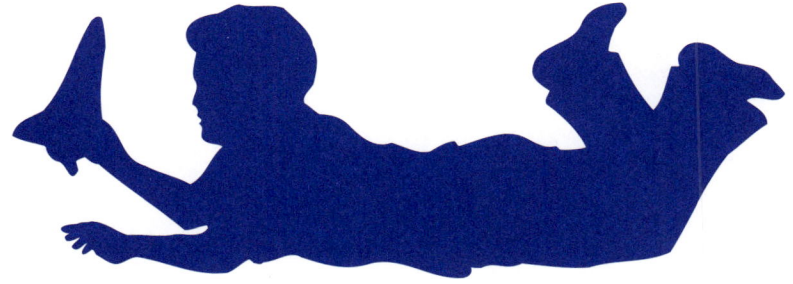

Remember that . . .

What you do as well as

what you don't do

can make a difference.

The question is . . .

How much of a difference

do you want to make?

—Duane Hodgin

Best of Character II ★ Published by The National Center for Youth Issues ★ 1-800-477-8277 ★ www.ncyi.org

# A New Catechism

Who is the pupil?

    A child of God, not a tool of the state.

Who is the teacher?

    A guide, not a guard.

What is the faculty?

    A community of scholars, not a union of mechanics.

Who is a principal?

    A master of teaching, not a master of teachers.

What is learning?

    A journey, not a destination.

What is discovery?

    Questioning the answers, not answering the questions.

What is the process?

    Discovering ideas, not covering content.

What is the goal?

    Opened minds, not closed issues.

What is the test?

    Being and becoming, not remembering and reviewing.

What is a school?

    Whatever we choose to make it.

—Allan A. Glatthorn

# Reach for the Power . . . . Teach

No other profession has the power.

The power to wake up young minds,

The power to wake up the world,

The power to truly make a difference

In the lives of young people.

You have the power...

ENERGIZE AND ENGAGE IT!

—Anonymous

Best of Character II ★ Published by The National Center for Youth Issues ★ 1-800-477-8277 ★ www.ncyi.org

# Teacher ....What do you make?

The dinner guests were sitting around the table discussing life. One man, a CEO, decided to explain the problem with education. He argued: "What's a kid going to learn from someone who decided his best option in life was to become a teacher?"

He reminded the other dinner guests that it is true what they say about teachers: "Those who can, do. Those who can't, teach."

To corroborate, he said to another guest: "You're a teacher, Susan," he said. "Be honest. What do you make?"

Susan, who had a reputation of honesty and frankness, replied, "You want to know what I make?"

"I make kids work harder than they ever thought they could. I can make a C+ feel like the Congressional Medal of Honor and an A- feel like a slap in the face if the student did not do his or her very best."

"I can make kids sit through 40 minutes of study hall in absolute silence."

"I can make parents tremble in fear when I call home."

"You want to know what I make?"

"I make kids wonder."
"I make them question."
"I make them criticize."
"I make them apologize and mean it."
"I make them write."
"I make them read, read, read."
"I make them spell 'definitely & beautiful' over and over again, until they will never misspell either one of those words again."
"I make them show all their work in math and hide it all on their final drafts in English."

"I elevate them to experience music and art and the joy in performance, so their lives are rich, full of kindness and culture, and they take pride in themselves and their accomplishments."

"I make them understand that if you have the brains, then follow your heart . . . And if someone ever tries to judge you by what you make, you pay them no attention."
"You want to know what I make?"
"I make a difference."

"What do you make?"

—Anonymous

# Molder of Dreams

*Shared with the 1986 Teacher of the Year, Guy Doud*
*By President Ronald Reagan*

Teachers, you are the molders of their dreams-
The gods who build or crush their young beliefs of
        Right……..and wrong
You are the spark that sets aflame the poet's hand,
    or lights the flame of some great singer's song.
You are the god of the young, the very young
You are the guardian of a million dreams.
Your every smile or frown can heal or pierce a heart.
Yours are a hundred lives, a thousand lives.
Yours is the pride of loving them and the sorrow, too.
Your patient work; your touch, make you the gods
of hope, Who fill their souls with dreams to make their
dreams come true.

—Clark Mollenhoff
Des Moines Register

# A Teacher's Prayer

Dear Lord, please help me—
To accept children as they are;
To recognize ability—and encourage it;
To understand shortcomings—and make allowances;
To work patiently for improvement;
To appreciate what children do right;
To be slow to anger and hard to discourage;
To demonstrate acts of kindness;
To be positive in thought;
To be willing to forgive and forget.
To be an example to others.

—Anonymous

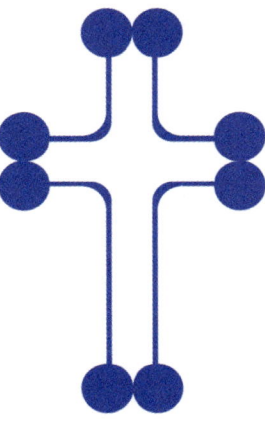

# Less We
# Not Forget

**In the interest of today's youth,**
We as adults must **forge ahead**
With the **constant understanding
and conviction** that
Through the **lives of the children
we teach and touch, our children,**
"the child in all of us" continues to live.

If these words are to ring true
And withstand the harshness of this world,
We must **always remember** that
**once upon a time,**
we were children too.
We must be willing to address our children's
**problems and possibilities,**
and **their hopes and fears,**
as if they were our own.

—Scott Samules

# THE DEMONSTRATION WAY

I'd rather see a lesson
Than to hear one any day.
I'd rather that you walk with me
Than to merely show the way.

The eye's a better teacher
And more willing than the ear
Your words can be confusing
But examples always clear.

The best of all the teachers
Are the ones who live the creed;
I care about my students
Is what everybody needs.

I soon can learn to do it
If you let me see it done.
I can see your hand in action
But your tongue too fast may run.

And the words that you are telling me
May be very fine and true,
But I'd rather get my lesson
By observing what you do.

—Anonymous

"I've come to a frightening conclusion that I am the decisive element in the classroom. It's my personal approach that creates the climate. It's my daily mood that makes the weather. As a teacher, I possess a tremendous power to make a person's life miserable or joyous. I can be a tool of torture or an instrument of inspiration. I can humiliate or humor, hurt or heal. In all situations, it is my response that decides whether a crisis will be escalated or de-escalated and a person humanized or de-humanized."

—Haim Ginott

# Sacred Work

A mind is a noble miracle—
potent, precious, and eager.

To enter and enhance such
architecture is sacred work.

To penetrate it is to caress
in motion infinite creation.

Though I shudder to know
my time is limited, still

I rejoice in the faith that
my influence is limitless.

To inspire is a privilege
I am blessed to pursue.

I am offered by providence
an immortality of touching.

I am a teacher—I touch
a thousand tomorrows today.

—Paris Goodrum

# Let It Begin With Me

The world's a disgrace and a terrible place.
Or at least say the prophets of doom.
With fear all around and no peace to be found,
It's a landscape of darkness and gloom.

There's hunger and doubt, and who cares about
All the suffering, trial and pain;
And there seems not a place in the whole human race
Where a soul can be happy again.

But that's not for me, for I can't help but see.
With the dawning of each brand new day,
That there's hope in the smile of every child,
And I just can't help feeling that way.

For the child of today is the person, they say,
Who will fashion the world that's to come;
and I know that I can in that life take a hand,
Shaping those who'll make tomorrow run.

So I pray that I'll reach every child I teach
With the finest that mankind can give,
And instill in these youth a life for the <u>truth</u>
Which will serve them wherever they live.

Let me teach them to know understanding and show
A <u>respect</u> for each person they see;
Let me teach them as they will teach others some day—
And let it begin with me!

—Anonymous

Best of Character II ★ Published by The National Center for Youth Issues ★ 1-800-477-8277 ★ www.ncyi.org

# The Teacher

Teaching is a special art,

You must have the skills, but it comes from the heart.

For teachers are special; they really care.

They give of themselves because they're willing to share.

Teaching the "basics", manners and values too,

They strive to bring out the best in you.


The demands are great; the rewards are few,

But the good teachers know what it is they do.

They make a difference, we never know how much.

In the hundreds upon hundreds of lives that they touch.


They are a role model for children that's easy to see,

They help children retain their dignity.

Their dedication is unswerving to the very end,

As a teacher, confidant, encourager and friend.


For teaching is a special art,

You must have the skills, but it comes from the heart.

—Anonymous

Listen to me

Even when I close my ears to you

Look at me

Even if I hide

Hold me

Even if I push you away

Laugh with me

Even if I cry

Love me

Even if I am unlovable

And please, please

Don't assume that I am all that I will ever be.

—Barb Roe

Best of Character II ★ Published by The National Center for Youth Issues ★ 1-800-477-8277 ★ www.ncyi.org

**Teaching is the oldest and most noble of professions.**

- **It is to be done well!**

- **It is to be done with enthusiasm!**

- **It is to be done with caring and dignity!**

—Duane Hodgin

# I am Important

I am an important part of this classroom;
I deserve to be treated with kindness and not
to be laughed at or teased.
I deserve not to be bullied, threatened,
pushed around, or to have my property
destroyed.
I deserve to express my opinions or ideas and
have them respected by others.
I deserve to learn and share my self with
others, and to express my feelings without
being criticized.
I deserve to be myself and be treated fairly. It
makes no difference how I look or think or
whether I am a boy or a girl.
I deserve to be respected as I respect
others.
I can be a friend, and I have a lot to offer in a
friendship: honesty, fun, sharing with one
another, caring for one another, and having
good feelings for one another.
I am important!

—Character Development Foundation

# Remember When?

*Remember when your mom bought your new pencils and notebooks?*
*When you had new school clothes?*
*And you were afraid you'd have*
*the school's meanest teacher?*
*Remember when you worried about finding the bathroom?*
*When you wondered if you'd ever find your bus?*
*And thought about your best friend*
*who wasn't in your class?*
*Remember when?*

*Remember when you had to write a story*
*on what you did over the summer vacation?*
*When you went to school and*
*couldn't find your new room?*
*And thought you'd never*
*make new friends again?*
*Remember when you got excited about*
*having new books assigned to you?*
*When you thought there was no way*
*you could eat lunchroom food?*
*And you wondered if the school*
*bully would pick on you this*
*year?*
*Remember when?*

*Remember when a teacher*
*Made a difference?*

—Patricia J. Anderson & Lester L. Laminack

A teacher is the "Guiding Light" in the "Search for Tomorrow" for the "Young and the Restless."

—Duane Hodgin

Best of Character II ★ Published by The National Center for Youth Issues ★ 1-800-477-8277 ★ www.ncyi.org

# Teacher's Prayer

I want to teach my students how to live this life on Earth, to face its struggles and its strife and improve their worth.

Not just a lesson in a book or how the rivers flow, but how to choose the proper path wherever they may go.

To understand eternal truth and know the right from wrong and gather all the beauty of a flower and a song.

For if I help the world to grow in wisdom and in grace, then I shall feel that I have won and I have filled my place.

And so I ask your guidance God, that I may do my part; for character and confidence and happiness of heart.

Amen

— James Metcalf

# Teaching

If I could . . .
    I would teach each child to be positive,
    to smile, to love and be loved.

    I would teach each child to take time
    to observe some miracle of nature—
    the song of a bird, the beauty of a snowflake,
    the orange glow of a winter sunset.

    I would teach each child to feel compassion
    toward the peers for whom the task of learning
    and the joys of life do not come easily.

    I would teach each one to be kind to all
    living creatures, including themselves,
    and to accept and respect the differences
    in all of us.

    I would teach each child that it is OK
    to show feelings by laughing, crying, or
    touching someone for whom he cares.

    Every day, each child would feel special,
    be courageous and, through my actions,
    each one would know how much I really care.

— Anonymous

**Courage**

**Teachers and Teaching**

Best of Character II ★ Published by The National Center for Youth Issues ★ 1-800-477-8277 ★ www.ncyi.org

# On Teaching

School is not easy, and it is not for the most part very much fun, but then, if you are very lucky, you may find a teacher. Three real teachers in a lifetime is the very best of luck. I have come to believe that a great teacher is a great artist, and that they are as few as there are any other great artists. Teaching might even be the greatest of the arts since the medium is the human mind and spirit.

My three had these in common—they all loved what they were doing. They did not tell—they catalyzed a burning desire to know. Under their influence, the horizons sprung wide and fear went away and the unknown became knowable. But most important of all, the truth, that dangerous stuff, became beautiful and precious.

—John Steinbeck

**Trust**

**Teachers and Teaching**

**SONGS & RAPS**

# Dr. Pep Character Rap

Yo, it's a hip-hop thing, take a look at my bling, bling. (2x)
Now listen up to what I say, Ya got to know about CIA. (2x)
If you want some satisfaction, you got to do some character in action. (2x)

Now my name is Dr. PEP, Ph.D. It may mean nothing to you but it is special to me. I'm a pretty exciting person. I'm a pretty hip dude. I try to be kind, I try not to be rude. I know what's right, I know what's good. I try to do the things that I know I should. Wherever I go, whomever I see, I try to make good character a part of me.

My character is important to me. It's what I do, It's what you see (2x)
Respect, trust and responsibility are a part of human dignity.

I say, R-E-S-P-E-C-T. It's up to you—it's up to me. (2x)

Now, E-X-A-M-P-L-E, is what we all strive to be. (2x)
I don't smoke and I don't drink, It's up to me what I choose to think. (2x)

I don't bully and I don't hurt. Cause those that do are nothing but jerks. (2x)
P-E-A-C-E, that spells Peace. It's up to you and me. (2x)

Now brotherhood and unity are part of P-E-A-C-E (That's PEACE! (2x))

You know what's right. You know what's good. Try to do the things that you know you should. Be good to yourself and others too, and you can be the best of you. (2x)

You know what's right, you know what's good. Do the things that you know you should. Be good to yourself and other too, and make good character (and peace) a part of you.

—Duane Hodgin

# Caring About Character Song

*(Tune of "Take Me out to the Ball Game")*

You know what's right so do it
each and every day
Be kind to others that you see.
Practice good manners and courtesy
Now, let's root, root, root for good character,
And use our "Ten Lifeskills" too.
It takes CAC (hand signs) to be good in our
homes and schools. (2x)

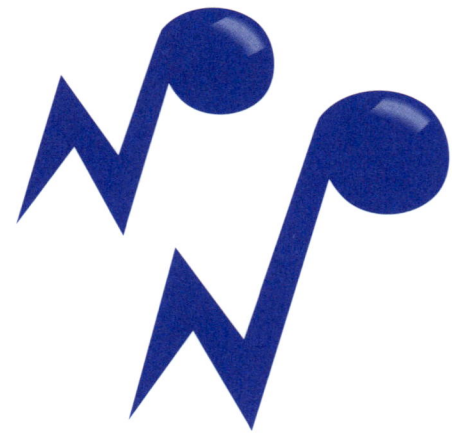

Best of Character II ★ Published by The National Center for Youth Issues ★ 1-800-477-8277 ★ www.ncyi.org

**M. S. D. of Lawrence Township
Diversity Presentation**

**D**ifferences
**I**ndividuals
**V**aluing
**E**veryone
**R**especting
**S**pecialness
**I**nclusion
**T**olerance
**Y**ou

## Diversity Song
(Rap or Poem)

**D-I-V-E-R-S-I** . . . give me a **T** and give me a **Y**
Put it **all together** and you will see
That it spells **Diversity!**
**Caring, accepting** and developing **trust**
Diversity is about **all of us.**

I am **different** and that's **OK!**
It makes **me special** in my own way.
I like me, and I like you
And together we have a job to do.

**Accepting others** like we know we should
That's the message of **brotherhood.**
So D-I-V-E-R-S-I . . . give me a T and give me a Y
In **diversity** we all **believe**
**Respect** and **uniqueness** we do **achieve.**

**So, be good to yourself and others too**
**And you can be the best of you.**

—Duane Hodgin

# RESPECT PARTICIPATION RAP

Respect — Respect — You've heard it
from some others. It's more than
just a word; it's the way we treat each other. (2x)

Respect — Respect — It's a two-way street.
When you give it and you get it,
it's really kind of neat. (2x)

Respect — Respect — Do it unto others.
Your parents, your teachers, your sisters
and your brothers. (2x)

R-E-S-P-E-C-T.
It helps to make a better me. (2x)

# CHARACTER

Character is who I am. It's part of me.
It's what I do and what others see.
Respect, Responsibility and genuine caring
It's serving others through helping and sharing.

Character is thinking about the things I say.
It's working with others in a cooperative way.
Honesty, Fairness, Truth and Trust
Help to bring out the good in all of us.

Character is strength and compassion too.
It can bring out the best in me and in you.
These are universal virtues to which we can
all relate.
It's a long habit continued, not dependent
upon fate.

Character is encouragement, a buffer in strife.
It gives us purpose and adds meaning to life.
Character counts in all that we do.
It must matter to me and matter to you.

For Character helps to make us whole.
It is the glue that binds our minds, spirits and souls.
Character is commitment; integrity it brings.
And It's having the courage to do the right things.

Yes, Character is part of me
It's what I do and what you see.

—Duane Hodgin

# Dr. Pep's Character Song

(Sung to the tune, "If You're Healthy and You're Happy")

If you are healthy and you are happy, clap your hands.
If you are healthy and you are happy, clap your hands.
If you are healthy and you are happy, then your life
will be quite snappy,
If you are healthy and you are happy, clap your hands.

If you try to do your best when you are in school, say I do.
If you try to do your best when you are in school, say I do.
If you try to do your best when you are in school,
that's a way to be "real cool"
If you try to do your best when you are in school, say I do.

If you know what's right and good, character handshake.
If you know what's right and good, character handshake.
If you know what's right and good, then you'll do
the things you should.
If you know what's right and good, character handshake.

If you are kind to others that you meet each day, give a smile.
If you are kind to others that you meet each day, give a smile.
If you are kind to others that you meet each day, then you say
these words with me
I like me, I like you, I will try to live the lifeskills and I hope that
you do too.
I like me, I like you, I will try to live the lifeskills and I hope that
you do too.

Now give me a "C - H - A - R - A - C - T - E - R!!
What's that spell?
So remember, be good to yourself and others too, and make
good character a part of you.

—Duane Hodgin

# Dr. Pep, Ph.D.'s Happy, Healthy, Helpful Song

(Sung to the tune, "If You're Healthy and You're Happy")

If you are healthy and you are happy,
clap your hands.
If you are healthy and you are happy,
clap your hands.
If you are healthy and you are happy,
then your life will be quite snappy,
If you are healthy and you are happy,
clap your thanks!

If you exercise and get your needed rest,
Flap your arms! (2x)
If you exercise and get your needed rest,
then you'll try to do your best.
If you exercise and get your needed rest,
Flap your arms!

If you eat nutritious food,
give the "Bump!" (2x)
If you eat nutritious food,
it will help improve your mood.
If you eat nutritious food,
give the "Bump!"

If you're kind to others that you meet each day,
say, "I'll try!" (2x)
If you're kind to others that you meet each day,
Then you'll say these words with me . . .

I like me, I like you, I try to have good character and
I hope that you do too! (2x)

—Duane Hodgin

BULLETIN BOARDS

# Cruzin' With Character

Decorate a bulletin board using the words "Cruzin' With Character" and images of automobiles traveling down the highway. On the side of each car, include life-skills that are needed to be a responsible person.

# Beacon of Good Character

Decorate a bulletin board with an image of a lighthouse labeled "Beacon of Good Character." From the lighthouse, show beams of light with words symbolizing the traits of responsibility (reliability, sense of duty, etc.)

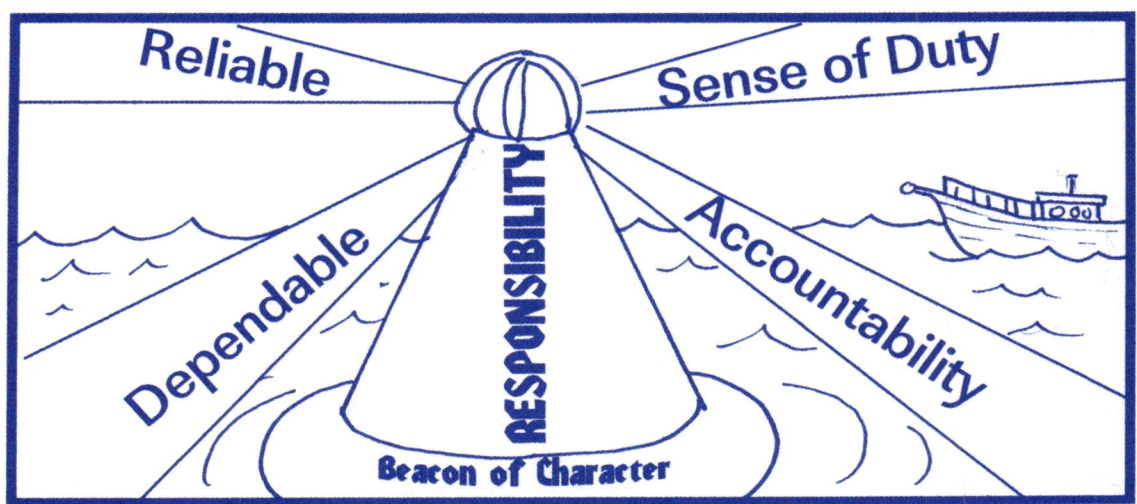

# Character in Action

Decorate a bulletin board using a picture of a young person being a good citizen or providing community service. Use the headline "Service is Character in Action" to emphasize the importance of the deed.

# We the People

Ask students to bring photos of themselves to class. Place the photos on the bulletin board around a drawing of the American flag. Underneath the photos the children can sign their name. At the top of the bulletin board is the title "We the People..." Underneath the flag, the slogan is complete with the words "...Support Citizenship."

# Road to Character

Decorate a bulletin board with a sun setting behind a hill and the word "Character" in the center of the sun. Along the road leading to the sun, place the words "Perseverance," "Endurance," "Strive," and "Goals" to symbolize some of the traits needed to attain good character. On the side of the road, create a sign with the phrase "Follow the yellow brick road to character."

# Character Heroes

Ask students to choose people that refused to give up until they reached their goal. It can be a person inside the school or a historical figure. Place images of the people on a bulletin board with a description on how they exemplify perseverance. Under the banner "Character Heroes," use the phrase "Perseverance: Never Give Up."

## Be the Best, Show Respect

Decorate a bulletin board using the theme "Be the Best, Show Respect." Add an image of two students working on a project together. Have one of the students complement the other on the work.

## It Begins with You and Me

Decorate a bulletin board using letters of the word "respect" on musical notes. Beneath the staff the notes are resting, use the phrase "It Begins and Ends with You and Me!"

# The Caring Connection

Decorate a bulletin board with a series of connected computers. On each monitor, place a student's photo emphasizing someone caring for another on the screen. Use the headline "Caring Connection."

## Important Words of Character

Decorate a bulletin board with the slogan "The Two Most Important Words in Character are Care and Act." Emphasize the words "care" and "act" by using different fonts and using arrows to direct attention.

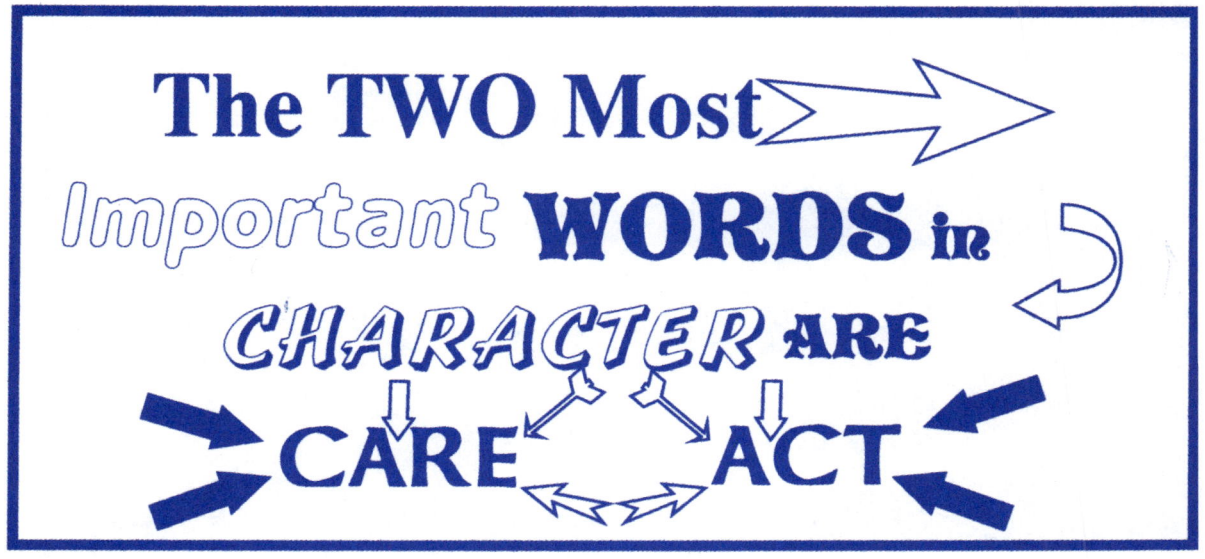

# Character Under Construction

Decorate a bulletin board with a brick wall missing a few bricks. Along the top of the wall, each brick will spell out the word "character." A few will be missing, however, to emphasize that character is always under construction and it takes courage to continue building the wall. In random bricks, will be tips to build a person's character.

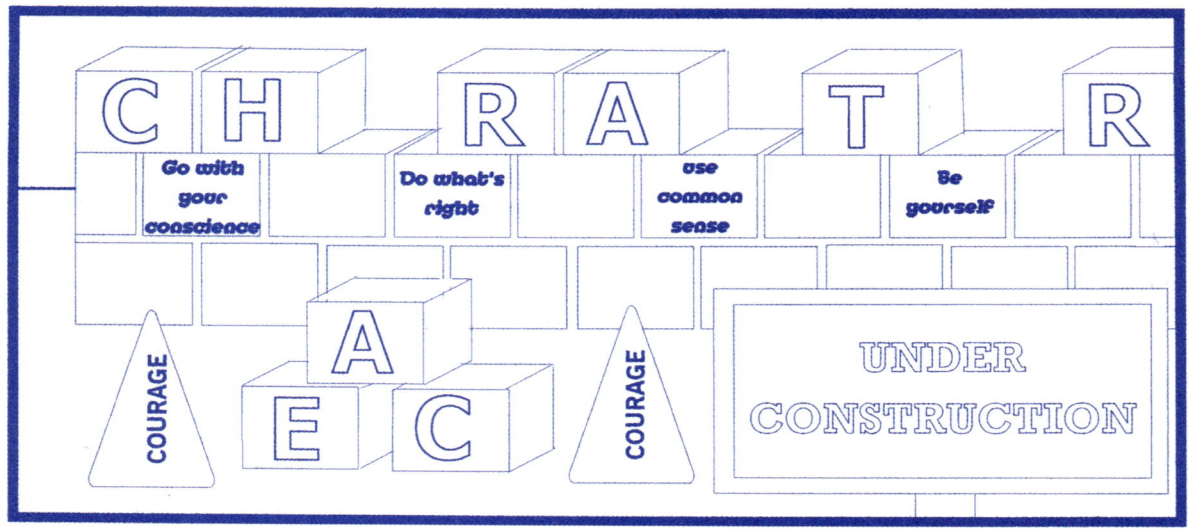

# Doing the Right Thing Takes Courage

Decorate a bulletin board with an image of a young person climbing out on a tree limb with a tip: Saying No to Drugs. Above and below the image use the title "Doing the Right Thing May Mean Going Out on a Limb!"

# Signs of Character

Decorate a bulletin board with street signs. On each sign are the slogans "Justice," "Fairness," and "Good Character." On two additional signs are the words "Stealing" and "Cheating" with a slash going through them to symbolize those traits are no acceptable.

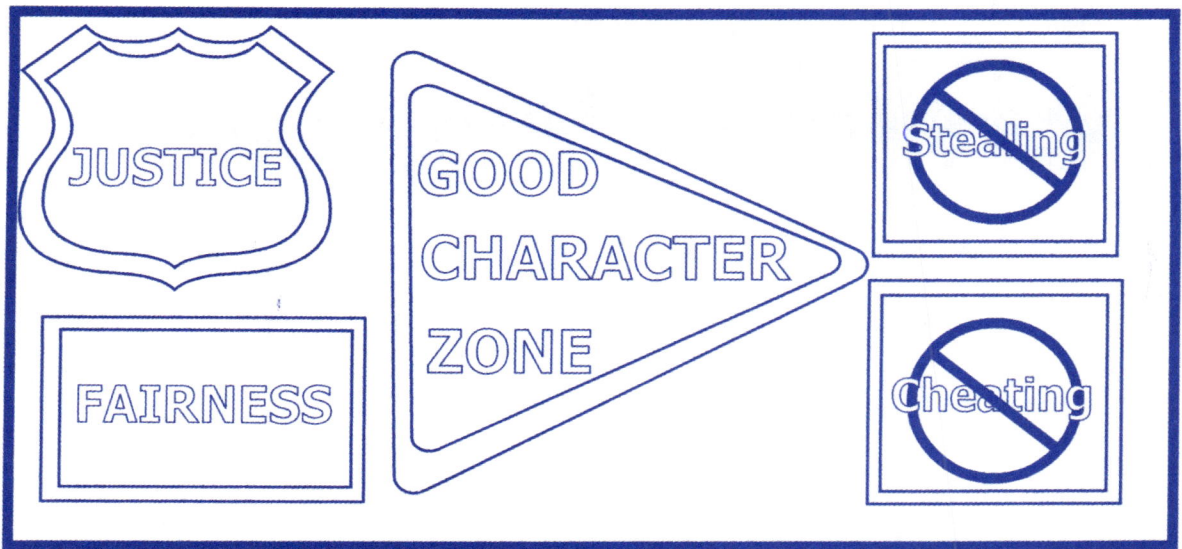

# Torches of Character

Decorate a bulletin board with torches and write character traits on the torches. Use the title "Good Character Lights Up Your Life."

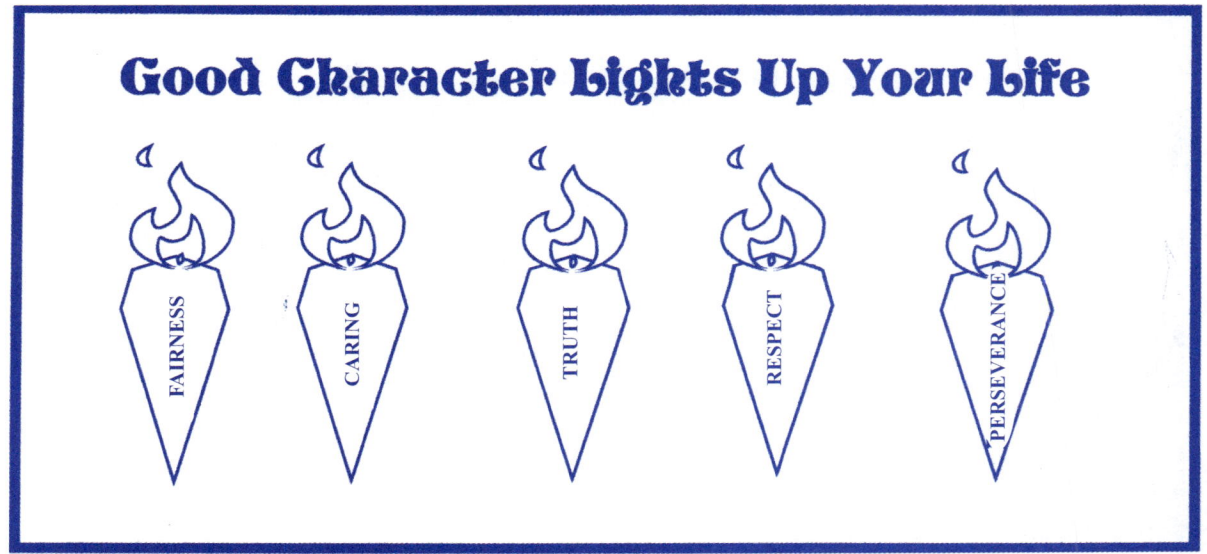

# We All Have a Story

Ask students to write a story about an experience or person in their life that emphasizes trust. Place the stories on the board with a picture or drawing of the person or event. Around the stories use the phrases "My Character, My Story" and "We all have a story. What's yours?"

# Strive to Be an Example

Decorate a bulletin board with images of children holding a sign. Together the signs spell the word "EXAMPLE." Underneath the children is the phrase "is what we ALL should strive to be!"